STANDARD ENGLISH SPEECH

T0382037

STANDARD
ENGLISH SPEECH

*A Compendium of English Phonetics for
Foreign Students*

BY

G. E. FUHRKEN, M.A. (Cantab.), Ph.D.

CAMBRIDGE
AT THE UNIVERSITY PRESS
1932

CAMBRIDGE
UNIVERSITY PRESS

University Printing House, Cambridge CB2 8BS, United Kingdom

Published in the United States of America by Cambridge University Press, New York

Cambridge University Press is part of the University of Cambridge.

It furthers the University's mission by disseminating knowledge in the pursuit of education, learning and research at the highest international levels of excellence.

www.cambridge.org
Information on this title: www.cambridge.org/9781107669109

© Cambridge University Press 1932

First published 1932
First paperback edition 2014

A catalogue record for this publication is available from the British Library

ISBN 978-1-107-66910-9 Paperback

CONTENTS

CONTENTS

PREFACE

The present compilation is mainly the product of the experience gained in teaching English to foreign students, especially those assembled from many countries during the last thirty years at Vacation courses in London and elsewhere.

In putting together my material I have omitted a number of minutiæ which, though not insignificant, seem to be too sporadic in their occurrence to be of general interest; this has enabled me to devote more space to phenomena that call for detailed elucidation. I have paid due deference to the opinions expressed in numerous books and articles on phonetics that have appeared in recent times, and have accepted such conclusions as tallied with my own as regards Standard speech.

Anyone who wishes to learn Standard English must hear it spoken, so this little volume can at most be a commentary on the living language in its spoken form. It attempts to show the foreign student where he is likely to go wrong, and how his mistakes may be rectified.

An earlier draft of this compendium was read by Dr Wilfrid Perrett, who suggested some additions to my exposition, criticized statements that were too loosely worded, and supplied me with some useful examples; I am much indebted to him for his scholarly help. Since then I have had sufficient leisure to recast the original draft throughout; in its revised form I ventured to submit it to Professor Otto Jespersen, who had the extreme kindness, despite the pressure of work following a period of convalescence after a serious illness, to read it and add some valuable marginal criticisms, which I have incorporated in the text or acknowledged in the foot-notes.

Before revising my MS. for the press I seized the opportunity offered me by Professor Daniel Jones of discussing with him several interesting phonetic questions on which we happen to hold different opinions, who gave me some useful suggestions and persuaded me to tone down a few assertions that were too dogmatically expressed. For devoting some hours of his valuable time to this discussion I beg to thank Professor Jones very sincerely; I much appreciate the benefit I derived from his long experience as a teacher of phonetics.

G. E. F.

London
   Aug. 1931

I

THE TRADITIONAL SPELLING
AND ITS DEFICIENCIES

1. The attempt to represent a spoken language by means of signs is very old. From picture-writing, as we know it from Egyptian records, a step forward was made when signs were invented to represent ideas. The Chinese have no alphabet, but some 40,000 syllabic characters, of which some 5000 are in common use.

2. A further advance was made when a separate symbol was adopted for each separate sound. Such writing was, roughly speaking, phonetic to start with, or at least it attempted to be. If this had continued, i.e. if spelling had been changed to keep pace with the changes that crept into the pronounced language from time to time, and new symbols had been adopted as the need for them arose, writing would be phonetic in languages where this principle had been rigorously carried out. In the case of English, the symbols that came to be adopted for the spelling were taken from the Latin alphabet, and the Latin alphabet was quite inadequate for the purpose.

3. A glance at the spelling of present-day English is sufficient to convince anyone with but a slight knowledge of the language that the spelling is far from being phonetic, even in the representation of what should be comparatively easy to deal with satisfactorily, viz. consonant-sounds. The same letter may represent several different sounds, as the *s* in *sign, easy, sure, measure*; the same sound may be represented by several different letters or combinations of letters, as the "hard *c*" sound in

cat, kill, lack, chord, quay; a letter may be written but not
sounded, as in the words *lamb, knife, whole, half, answer*. And
so on. A complete list of these and other inconsistencies would
fill pages of print. In short, the ordinary English spelling is
bewildering. Innumerable words are still clothed, so to speak,
in a medieval robe. And one of the chief causes of this conservatism, curiously enough, was the invention of printing. The
printers gradually adopted a uniform spelling, and forced it on
the public. Deviations from printers' spelling came to be regarded as incorrect. The last vestiges of variation in spelling
practically disappeared with the publication of Johnson's
Dictionary in 1755.

4. Meanwhile the pronunciation kept changing and is still
changing; and thus it has come about that words are written
in an obsolete and misleading manner. The time that has to
be devoted to teaching children to spell is only one of the dis-
advantages of our conventional way of representing words in
writing; but it is the one most readily acknowledged by members of the teaching profession, to whom it is constantly being
brought home.

5. Proposals for reforming this state of things have been
under discussion for many years. The Spelling Reform Association and the Simplified Spelling Board in U.S.A., and the
Simplified Spelling Society in England, have suggested a number
of reforms, ranging from the radical one of entirely rewriting
the language on phonetic lines to the system of introducing
changes gradually, so as not to shock the prejudices of those
who were accustomed to the eccentricities of the existing mode
of spelling words. But even these minor improvements en-
countered so much opposition, and aroused so little interest,
that the prospects of ever accomplishing anything in the way

of reform looked exceedingly gloomy. The difficulties were intensified by the different aims of the various reformers.

6. An ingenious compromise was effected in 1930 by Professor Zachrisson of Uppsala, who had set himself the task of retaining the Roman alphabet, using and combining its symbols in a consistent way, making its symbols serve phonetic ends, and yet evolving a new orthography which would bear sufficient resemblance to the present spelling for the two systems to be used side by side for the same purpose. After several consultations with a number of English and American experts on spelling reform, he brought out *Anglic; a New Agreed Simplified English Spelling*. In a brochure[1] which explains the principles and spelling rules of "Anglic" he states: "If Anglic is taught, at least as an optional subject, in all continental Elementary Schools, if courses are arranged for adults to learn it all over the world...we shall have solved the problem of an international language".

7. "Anglic" is without doubt the best solution of the spelling problem for beginners in English that has hitherto appeared. Its greatest merits are that it has utilized the most common or serviceable of the existing spelling variants, and, by leaving about forty of the commonest words unchanged as fixed forms or *word-signs* to be memorized, has evolved a spelling reform that is phonetic in principle and yet leaves from 60 per cent. to 75 per cent. of the words on an average printed page unchanged. The transition from "Anglic" spelling to ordinary spelling is remarkably easy, as has been proved by practical tests. "It does not favour either the British or the American Standard Pronunciation, but can be used in New York as well as in London, in Aberdeen as well as in San Francisco."

[1] *Anglic*, by R. E. Zachrisson. Anglic Fund A.B.: Uppsala, 1930.

8. But though "Anglic" may have provided a satisfactory solution of one aspect of spelling reform, there remains the question whether the traditional spelling cannot be improved in some particulars where it is unnecessarily clumsy or misleading. Thus, it is impossible in script or print to indicate, by the orthodox spelling, the difference between *I read*, present tense, and *I read*, past tense. The same blundering use of a digraph to represent a short vowel-sound may also be seen in the word *dreamt*, a stupid blend of the two forms that existed in early modern English, *dremt* and *dreamed*. Similarly, the forms *dealt*, *leant*, *leapt*, *meant* could well be supplanted by *delt*, *lent*, *lept*, *ment*. Or again, why not keep the alternative spelling *decad* for *decade*; the latter often elicits the faulty pronunciation which makes it a homonym of *decayed*.

9. "Anglic" forms a convenient stepping-stone between the hopelessly unphonetic nomic spelling and a phonetic spelling. But "Anglic" is not strictly phonetic; thus, for instance, it writes *far* for a word that has quite a number of different pronunciations in different parts of the English-speaking world. In dealing with sounds *per se* we must therefore employ symbols that are not liable to be interpreted in several different ways. This will save us as much trouble as the use of figures in dealing with a mathematical problem. On the other hand, we cannot ignore the nomic spelling, for it exercises a marked influence on the pronunciation of words that are not in common use, one result of which is the formidable list of disputed pronunciations in English speech.

10. A spelling reform that still awaits an influential advocate is wanted for the names given to the letters of the English alphabet. The English child hears certain sounds in the word *you*, and is taught to associate those sounds with the letters of

the alphabet which go under the names of "why, owe, you". No wonder that children find spelling so confusing! The reformer who sets out to rechristen the letters might do worse than take a hint from the signallers' alphabet, in which *p.m.* is referred to as "pip emma". This, at any rate, would be a step in the right direction.

11. An investigation of the spoken sounds of a language can only be based on the sounds themselves, and a study of the sounds entails a knowledge of what speech-organs are used to produce the sounds, and a conception of how those sounds are produced.

12. To state that a child can imitate sounds and produce them adequately without being conscious of how it forms them is no argument against the study of phonetics. We have only to remember how long and laboriously the child has been hearing them and practising them before they become anything like perfect. Even so, the child has acquired but a very limited number of speech-sounds. The student of languages must extend his researches very much more widely than a child who only requires a primitive vocabulary.

13. But here we must set a limit. The sounds of any given language are almost innumerable if regard is paid to all the class variations that can be heard, to all the dialects that are spoken, and to all the individual peculiarities that exist. We must therefore confine ourselves in the main to such sounds as are essential to the speech of educated people in its most acceptable form, which means in the form freest from dialect characteristics. If we do this we may assume that the sounds of the language are limited, and that a limited number of symbols will suffice to represent them.

II

THE STUDY OF PHONETICS.
PHONETIC SYMBOLS

14. The study of phonetics has from its earliest infancy found a fertile field in England. The father of the movement may be said to have been Alexander John Ellis (1814–90), whose *Essentials of Phonetics* (1848) was the first learned contribution to the subject in modern times. In 1867 came Alexander Melville Bell's *Visible Speech*, a masterpiece of observation, but a book that can only appeal to the advanced student. The first publication that helped to popularize the study of phonetics, and at the same time to introduce it into the class-room, was Henry Sweet's *Elementarbuch des gesprochenen Englisch* (1885). A further stimulus was given by Laura Soames's *An Introduction to Phonetics* (1891), and more recently by the publications of Walter Ripman (*The Sounds of Spoken English*), Daniel Jones (*The Pronunciation of English*), and others.

15. It was in France, however, that the idea originated of drawing up an international alphabet in which each symbol should have a definite scope. The intention was, in the first place, to simplify the study of sounds by supplying a practical alphabet that could serve to transcribe a large number of modern languages and dialects. Its originator, Paul Passy, succeeded in bringing a certain measure of uniformity where previously there had been divergence and consequent confusion. Thanks to his initiative, the "International Phonetic Association" became an influential authority in the sphere of practical phonetics.

16. The following phonetic symbols are required for a very broad transcription of English sounds:

ɑː as in	half, card	i as in	six, hid
ai ,,	life, five	iː ,,	three, bead
au ,,	thousand, house	ou ,,	note, code
æ ,,	cat, bad	ɔ ,,	not, cod
ei ,,	eight, bayed	ɔː ,,	four, cord
ɛ ,,	ten, bed	ɔi ,,	boy, oil
ɛə ,,	air, bared	ʌ ,,	some, cud
ə ,,	among, stirrup	u ,,	put, could
əː ,,	third, murmur	uː ,,	two, cooed
j as in	yes	ʃ as in	ship, wish
ð ,,	this, paths	tʃ ,,	church
θ ,,	thin, path	ʒ ,,	vision, pleasure
ŋ ,,	sing, ink	ʤ ,,	pigeon, judge

The other consonant-symbols as the italicized letters in babe, dad, fife, gag, he, kiosk, lily, mum, nine, pope, rest, dress, taught, vest, west, zest.

Stress is usually marked by placing a sign, preferably a perpendicular line, before the stressed syllable (dis'kriːt).

17. The symbols shown above are those required for transcribing English if we merely desire to indicate approximately the pronunciation of the language in its most acceptable form. The same symbols, with slightly different values as a rule, can be utilized in transcribing other languages, and fresh symbols adopted for sounds quite foreign to English. The practical advantages that the I.P.A. phonetic alphabet possesses over other systems of transcription have been much appreciated throughout the world, and the I.P.A. symbols are in general use to-day.

18. Of the many rival systems, each with its particular advantage or advantages, the best known is Sweet's "Broad Romic", which has been used in many text-books published abroad. The great advantage of this system is that it is so easily written and printed, but this advantage was gained at the expense of consistency. Thus, Sweet used doubled letters to indicate some of the long vowels, and not others; i.e. he wrote *farm* (**faam**), but *caught* (**kɔt**); he used the same symbol in English *but* and German *Bad* (**bat**), though the two vowels are not varieties of one and the same vowel-sound; he used **o** for the vowel in *not* (**not**) and for the first element of the diphthong heard in *note* (**nout**). These inconsistencies were confusing to the pupil, and became still more confusing when some additional language had to be dealt with, such as French.

Moreover, the use of doubled letters to indicate long sounds violates the principle of using one symbol for one sound, which is one of the ideals a phonetic alphabet should keep in view.

19. These are the chief reasons why Sweet's "Broad Romic" is now generally discarded, and the symbols of the I.P.A. used in its place. From the list of symbols required for a Broad transcription of English, as given in § 16, it will be seen that some forty symbols are required to indicate roughly the commonest sounds used in educated speech. As a great number of the consonant-symbols correspond with the letters of the alphabet in their commonest values, little time is required to master so simple a system; the ultimate saving in time and labour, both for teacher and pupil, is very considerable.

20. The Broad notation of the I.P.A. has this in common with other simple graphic systems: it prefers to omit many details rather than become too scientific for practical purposes. One of these is the comparative length of vowel- and consonant-

sounds. Thus, it uses a length-mark to indicate vowels that are usually long or half-long, and no mark for vowels that are generally short or half-long; and this rough and ready method of marking vowel-length has to suffice in the elementary stages of learning a foreign language. For consonant-sounds no length-marks are used, though consonants vary considerably in length; thus, the *n* at the beginning of the word *not* is shorter than at the end of the word *man*, and the *n* is still longer in the word *hand*. These differences must be ignored in a simple transcription, though it may occasionally prove necessary to correct pronunciation by having recourse to the length-mark ː, as in the last example, and put the transcription with the length-mark inserted upon the blackboard (hænːd), in order to draw attention to this point. In teaching English to Swedes and Norwegians it is seldom necessary to indicate the length of consonant-sounds, as the quantity of consonant-sounds runs closely parallel in the speech of these peoples.[1] Far greater difficulties in this domain are presented by the mistakes that Germans and Danes naturally make when they begin to study English: they must first learn to lengthen consonant-sounds in positions where they are inclined to pronounce them short; cf. English *lamb*, with its long final m, with German *Lamm*, that has a short m.

21. Another point with which a simple transcription cannot concern itself is to indicate that the place of articulation of some sounds differs markedly from the one generally employed in the majority of such languages as are most commonly studied. Thus, English t is produced much further back than in most other languages—so far back, indeed, that children confuse it

[1] If we except the doubled consonants; cf. English *hammer* with Swedish *hammare*.

with **k** when it is followed by I, and say **likl** for **litl**.[1] In one and the same language a consonant may be differently articulated according to the vowel that follows it, as in *kill* and *cool*; the former is pronounced with a "front" **k**, the latter with a "back" **k**. If one kept a front **k** before **uː** in *cool*, one would be apt to insert a glide between the two, as is done in the word *cure* (**kjuɜ**), or in the older pronunciation of *car*, i.e. **kjɑː**, still occasionally to be heard in provincial speech (see also § 203).

22. Another thing a simple transcription does not attempt to record, is the energy with which a sound is produced. For instance, an English f is articulated with more energy than a German f: cf. English *felt* with German *Feld*. The former could be transcribed **fʰɛlt** if we wanted to accentuate this difference, assuming for the moment that the other sounds are identical, which they are not.

23. So also with lip-rounding. The extent to which the lips are rounded is, in fact, almost impossible to indicate. It is well to remember, however, that lip-rounding is much less marked in English than in most European languages (cf. what is said in § 59 about unrounded **o**).

24. Then there is the question of intonation, i.e. the constantly changing pitch of the musical note produced by the vocal cords, the elastic ligaments stretched across the interior of the larynx (cf. § 43). This is exceedingly difficult to indicate, and, at the best, can only be shown very imperfectly. Phonetic texts generally ignore intonation, the chief reason being the difficulty of printing intonation lines, and the cost of producing texts which include them; apart from the expense of setting up the type, they add very considerably to the space occupied by it. Those interested in the subject should consult Professor Daniel

[1] See O. Jespersen, *Lehrb. d. Phon.* p. 171.

Jones's *Intonation Curves* (published 1909, by Teubner), a collection of phonetic texts in which the intonation is marked throughout by means of curved lines on a musical stave. A later work, dealing more fully with the intricacies of the subject, is by H. Klinghardt (see Bibliography). The devices in this volume for marking stress and intonation are extremely simple and easily interpreted.

25. But even if we disregard such niceties as intonation, energy, and lip-rounding, we may find the Broad transcript unsatisfactory in several respects when we discuss the sounds of a language in detail, or compare them with the sounds of other languages. We are compelled to use a Narrow (more exact) transcript, one form of which is employed in the following sections, in so far as exactitude is called for.

Without discussing in this place the advantages to be gained by using a more exact transcript than the Broad, we may select two instances to show that the Broad transcript will not suit our purpose. The Broad forms biːd and bit for *bead* and *bit* suggest that the two vowels differ only in length, and not in quality; but the former is "tense" as compared with the latter (see § 47). Now this tense vowel can be shortened, as in *beat*, the lax vowel lengthened, as in *bid*, in which case the difference in length becomes negligible. But the difference in quality remains. A Frenchman naturally substitutes a short tense i for the English lax sound, i.e. the quality of his vowel differs from the one required for the English sound. In other words, we must have a separate symbol for the vowel in *bit* and *bid*. For this we will adopt ɪ, which is the letter *I* in its smaller form (small capital).

So also for the vowel-sounds in *food* and *foot*, *coot* and *could*. The tense vowel in *coot* may be as short as the lax vowel in *could*, as we shall discover later on. Scotsmen frequently use a short tense vowel, making the u in *food* as short as the English vowel in *foot*, but with a vowel that differs from it in quality. For the sound in *foot*, *could* we therefore require a separate symbol, and can take the small form of the capital *U*.

26. For the Broad symbols ei and ou it has been thought expedient to substitute e^i and o^u in the sections following, to show that the i and u in ei and ou are not integral elements, as are the i and u in the true diphthongs ai and au heard in *like* and *how*. In Northern E. eː and oː are more generally in use than the diphthongal forms heard in Southern E., while even in Southern E. the vowels are not diphthongized when immediately followed by an unstressed vowel, as in *laity* (leˑɪtɪ), *poetry* (poˑɪtrɪ), nor always before a voiceless consonant, as in *relation* (rɪˈleˑʃn), *emotion* (ɪˈmoˑʃn), nor as a rule in unstressed syllables, as in *chaotic* (keˈɒtɪk), *November* (noˈvɛmbɜ).

For Broad and Narrow symbols, see § 50.1.

27. It is now generally agreed that the first thing to be studied in learning a living language is, not the higher literary form of it, but the conversational form as spoken by educated people. The best preparation for this is to study the principles of phonetics as applicable to one's own language; having thus gained a sure phonetic basis on which to build up, the student can pass on to a foreign language. He will find that he has to acquire a number of sounds that are lacking in his own set of speech-sounds, or only faintly resemble them, and he will have to practise them diligently until he has mastered them. At this stage of his studies he should use a phonetic transcription of the foreign language to the exclusion of the traditional spelling. The transcription already solves a number of difficulties, and a good teacher will explain the faulty formation of sounds

and the incorrect intonation, etc. that stand in the way of the student's pronunciation being like a standard pronunciation. Where native teachers are not available, as in outlying country districts, the best substitute[1] for them is good gramophone records to accompany phonetic texts. But with a gramophone the process is not so simple, for the same record must be repeated innumerable times before the pupil has mastered it, so that a course of gramophone lessons is of little use to an impatient student, or to one whose powers of imitation are poor, for he may fondly believe he has mastered a text and can faithfully reproduce it, when as a matter of fact he has only managed to gabble off something that would be almost incomprehensible to anyone else. We must not expect too much of a medium like the gramophone, which cannot answer the simplest of questions, or give advice at the moment when it is urgently needed. Any substitute of this kind for the trained teacher is at best a *faute de mieux*—and this applies with still greater force to broadcast lessons, especially for beginners.

III

VARIETIES OF SPOKEN ENGLISH

28. It is a well-known phenomenon that people living in the same geographical area are inclined to have common peculiarities in speaking their own or a foreign language. Climatic and atmospheric conditions can, perhaps, be made accountable for some of these local peculiarities. Thus, people living near the sea-border are prone to nasalize; this is noticeable along the

---

[1] Assuming, of course, that there is no trained phonetician to take his place.

east coast of Scotland, in Holland, Friesland, and along the west coast of Norway and Sweden, but not on the east coast of Sweden. The percentage of salinity in the air may lie at the root of the matter. Such nasalizing is different in origin from the imitated nasalizing that may spread over the greater part of a country. Imitation is the most potent factor in bringing about sound-changes. But certain speech peculiarities may derive from such causes as the effect on the organs of speech produced by a very dry or very moist climate, by living in crowded towns—with their dust and smoke—by extremes of heat and cold, by local affectations of speech, national temperament—indolence, excitability, nonchalance, impatience—distance from centres of culture, and influences exerted by other languages spoken in neighbouring districts. How far hereditary influences extend, it is impossible to know; but in this connection it is noticeable how the English of the areas where the Angles settled is still clearly differentiated from that of the Saxon settlements.

29. It is naturally easier to learn a language that is cognate to one's own than one that is not. Scandinavians, Dutchmen and Frisians should therefore speak English with a better accent than Frenchmen, Russians, or Hungarians. The more closely cognate the languages are, the fewer will be the difficulties that present themselves. An Icelander has great advantages over a Prussian in learning English, a Prussian over a Parisian, and so forth. Broadly speaking, the best linguists are the members of nations that have to speak two or more languages. Within one and the same nation, those who speak their own tongue with the purest accent learn other tongues best. Germans with marked dialect peculiarities pronounce English badly; those from the north-west of the dominion pronounce it well.

30. The form of English that foreigners endeavour to acquire is generally spoken of as Standard English.[1] By this is meant the form of it employed by educated people in the home counties, i.e. the counties nearest to the capital, and particularly the educated speech of Londoners. This is the form of spoken English which is freest from provincial features, and is the form which other speakers of English in Great Britain endeavour to acquire. It is prevalent in the south-east of England, and is spreading rapidly to the north and west. The geographical nursery of St. E. could be roughly drawn on the map by marking a line from Warwick running due east, and another running due south. West of the perpendicular line is the domain of Western E.; north of the horizontal line begins the domain of Northern E., with its characteristic features becoming clearly marked in the more northerly parts of the Midlands.

31. Northern E. differs from St. E. in having purer, i.e. fewer diphthongal, vowels. It substitutes other vowel-sounds for those heard in the St. E. pronunciation of *glass*, *man*, *but*. Actually it represents an older form of English. It is also characterized by having "coronal" vowels (§ 127), and fewer weak forms in unstressed syllables.

A subdivision of it is the dialect of Durham and Northumberland, where the pronunciation is drawling and monotonous, and nearly as "broad" as in Scotland. One of its local peculiarities is the uvular r, as in Parisian French, often called the "Northumbrian burr" (see §§ 45 and 123).

32. The Western dialect can be heard most clearly in Somerset and Devonshire. One of its chief features is the substitution of voiced for voiceless consonants, as in zum for *some* (sʌm),

---

[1] The contraction "St. E." stands for "Standard English" in the pages following.

vox for *fox*; hence the regular English form *vixen* for a she-fox. Coronal vowel-sounds are common, and more marked than in Northern E. Another feature is a very "advanced" form of uː, as in *poodle*, reminiscent of French **u**. The nearer we get to the Welsh border, the more the speech of the natives shows the influence of Keltic intonation and rapidity of articulation. The Dorsetshire form of Western E. can be studied in the works of Thomas Hardy (1840–1928) and the poetry of William Barnes (1801–86).

33. In and around London there is the dialect of the lower classes, known as "cockney". This is the least conservative of all forms of English, and is in a continual state of rapid flux. It even anticipates changes that ultimately force their way into St. E., and is thus valuable in showing tendencies of development. For instance, the word *house*, which was pronounced **huːs** in the Early English period, and subsequently passed through various intermediate stages, is now **hæus** or **haːs** in cockney speech, and one of these last may ultimately become the Standard form. Similarly *time*, once pronounced **tiːmə**, is now **taim** in St. E., and may be heard as **taim** or **tɔim** in cockney dialect.

34. Cockney speech is by no means confined to the capital: it may be heard commonly in Essex and Kent, and extends north into Cambridgeshire and Bedfordshire. It may even be doubted whether cockney speech originated in the capital; there is absolutely no proof that it did. And since, quite recently, the pronunciation of the cockney himself has vastly improved, thanks to the spread of elementary education, cockney speech clings more tenaciously to the Essex countryside than to London proper. If, as some believe, Essex was the first home of cockney, from where it spread to the other home counties,

Essex may also prove to be its last biding-place. But the whole problem bristles with difficulties, and no scholar of English has hitherto made it a subject of special study. Moreover, the material for a study of its earlier phases is lacking. So, possibly, an important chapter in the development of St. E. can never be written.

35. The foreigner who wishes to study English will obviously prefer to base his studies on that form of it which educated people aim at in England itself, and avoid dialect forms. He will confine himself, therefore, to the study of St. E. in the matter of pronunciation.

36. Though an attempt has been made above to define what is meant by St. E., it must always be remembered that no two persons pronounce exactly alike. The St. E. pronunciation of any given word is really the form it assumes at a given time in the speech of the majority of educated people who have acquired their pronunciation through the medium of frequent intercourse with educated speakers of St. E.

37. An answer to the question "Where is the best English spoken?" was given in 1927 by one of the most distinguished linguists in England, as follows: "The best English in the world is taught on the London stage and talked in the great London clubs". Sir Denison Ross went on: "There is no doubt that the London stage has done much to set and preserve the standard pronunciation of English, but I must say that I fear to contemplate what will happen if many more American plays come to London. Of late years American slang expressions have been introduced into the English language at an alarming rate, especially since in this country the American style of advertising was adopted. Yet I think that, like once-popular songs, slang words that are forced into the English language will have their

day and pass away more rapidly than they can pass into the new dictionaries.

"In my opinion it is the middle-aged clubmen of London who are the true guardians of the best-spoken English, while the best-written English is preserved in the leader columns of our foremost newspapers. I say 'middle-aged' clubmen, because young men of all classes are influenced by the slang of the day, but by the time young clubmen reach middle age they will have ceased to use slang words—they will have become self-conscious about using them. Slang is youthful!" And with that verdict few people will be inclined to disagree.

38. There is a tendency in some quarters to find fault with the term St. E., and to substitute for it other terms, such as "The King's English", "Public School English", "Received English", etc.[1]

But there is no reason why the commonly accepted expression "Standard English" should not be retained, provided that it is interpreted in conformity with the definition given in § 30. This is a definite and recognized type of spoken English with which comparisons may conveniently be made.[2]

39. Every language has its "standard" pronunciation, or

[1] By "The King's English" is generally understood the correct written form of the language, grammatically viewed, as practised by the best authors. "Public School English" is an unsatisfactory term, seeing that certain mannerisms find a home in the public schools from time to time (see § 133). The correct use of the term "Received English" can be seen in Thomas Hardy's Preface (1898) to *Wessex Poems*: "Whenever an ancient and legitimate word of the district, for which there was no equivalent in received English, suggested itself as the most natural, nearest, and often only expression of a thought, it has been made use of, on what seemed good grounds".

[2] The chief objectors to the term St. E. are educated speakers who retain some dialect peculiarities. But they should bear in mind that you can't get rid of a wart by calling it a pimple.

something approximating to it. In comparing two languages
it is necessary to take the "standard" forms of these languages;
this will save confusion. A foreigner's pronunciation of an
English word may be English without being St. E., and will
need correction. Thus, if we hear a Norwegian pronounce the
word *poodle* with his own u sound, it is better to correct him
than to tell him that his vowel resembles the one frequently
heard in Devonshire. For if we were to admit as allowable
every variety of pronunciation that our dialects disclose, we
should have to call almost any form of pronunciation more or
less correct. A Yorkshireman may say "Tak yer wull o't",
meaning "Take what you will out of it", i.e. "Help yourself".
But a foreigner would not care to set that up as his conception
of normal English. All dialects are full of poetry, history and
music; they have a life of their own; but we must relegate them
to their proper place.

IV

SOUND, AND THE ORGANS OF SPEECH

40. Sound is not only the sensation produced through the
organs of hearing, but also the physical cause of this sensation.
In the case of linguistic sounds the sensation produced is more
or less clear, the physical cause more or less obscure. Though
we recognize a sound as one with which we are familiar, we
may be quite ignorant of how that sound is produced. By
watching people speak we see how lips and possibly the point
of the tongue take up positions that are evidently essential to
the production of certain sounds. The other physical causes are
hidden from the eye, and even a looking-glass does not help

much to reveal them. Unless we go beyond this stage we remain mere imitators of sounds, and have only a vague idea of how one sound is made distinguishable from another. We must therefore investigate how linguistic sounds are produced.

41. It is true that we may be able to produce a sound correctly and yet be unconscious of our phonetic mechanism, just as it is true that we may be perfectly conscious of that mechanism and yet be unable to produce a sound correctly; but, other things being equal, it is self-evident that the more we know about linguistic sounds and how they should be produced the more likely we are to pronounce correctly. A sound which is at once correctly and consciously formed is a much safer acquisition than a merely successful imitation in the production of which we are ignorant of how the organs of speech are being adjusted. We must at least have an elementary knowledge of how and where speech-sounds are produced.

42. Speech-sounds are produced by air which, forced from the lungs through the windpipe, is affected in its subsequent passage by the organs of speech, of which the chief are the *larynx, glottis, pharynx, uvula, nasal cavity* and *mouth*.

43. The larynx is situated at the upper part of the windpipe, and consists of a cartilaginous box across which are stretched folds of mucous membrane, the edges of which, the vocal cords, produce sound, or voice, when vibrated. The space between the cords is called the glottis. When the glottis is closed, breath is stopped; when partially closed, voice is produced; when open, breath alone results. Voiced sounds are therefore those produced with vibration of the vocal cords; such are, all normally sounded vowel-sounds, and some of the consonants (see § 108 *seq.*).

The epiglottis, a cartilaginous lid, shaped like a leaf, and situated at the base of the tongue, closes the larynx during the

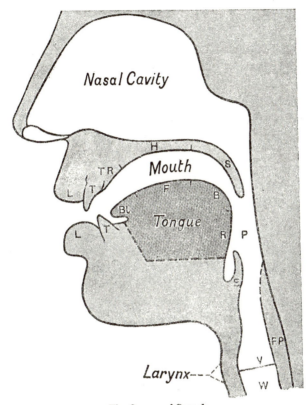

The Organs of Speech.

From Daniel Jones's *The Pronunciation of Russian.*

(Reproduced with the author's permission.)

B. Back of Tongue.   *Bl.* Blade of Tongue.   *E.* Epiglottis.   *F.* Front
of Tongue.   *FP.* Food Passage.   *H.* Hard Palate.   *LL.* Lips.
P. Pharyngeal Cavity (Pharynx).   *R.* Root of Tongue.   *S.* Soft
Palate.   *TT.* Teeth.   *TR.* Teeth-Ridge.   *V.* Position of Vocal
Cords.   *W.* Windpipe.

act of swallowing, but plays no part in the production of normal speech-sounds.

44. The quality of the voice is modified in the supraglottal passages, which form a resonance chamber; they consist of the pharynx (between the epiglottis and uvula), the nasal cavity and the mouth. The pharynx serves as both air-passage and food-passage. But the beauty of voiced sounds depends very greatly on the resonance of the vocal cords.

45. The uvula, or pendent flabby portion of the soft palate, can close either the opening from the pharynx to the nasal passages, or the opening from the pharynx to the mouth. The uvula can moreover be made to vibrate, as in the production of the so-called "uvular *r*". When the passage to the nose is left open, by lowering the uvula, the organs of speech are adjusted for the production of clear nasal tones.

46. The mouth contains the tongue, the soft and hard palates, gums, teeth and lips. The "back" of the tongue is the part opposite the soft palate when the tongue is at rest, the "front" the part opposite the hard palate, the "blade" the part touching the gums. The "blade" includes the "tip". Note that the blade of the tongue plays a large part in forming consonants, an insignificant one in forming vowels.

47. The character of a vowel-sound is determined by various factors, of which the most important for purposes of classification are these:

(1) the place of articulation in the mouth, and the movement of that part of the tongue which is instrumental in helping to articulate the sound;

(2) the relative tenseness or laxness assumed by lips, cheeks, tongue and pharynx while the sound is being produced;

generally speaking, tenseness or laxness is not confined to one organ of speech, but shared;

(3) the rounding, spreading, or passiveness of the lips and oral cavity; lip-rounding necessarily includes the cheeks, while inner rounding affects the shape of the pharynx.

It will simplify our classification of the vowels if we confine ourselves to a consideration of these three main factors. The two latter are fairly easy to determine; not so with the first. Here aural and visual impressions do not take us far; we must draw on the results obtained hitherto by experimental methods. We can then class the vowels and name them from their manner of formation.

48. When the tongue rises towards the hard palate to almost the highest possible approach without producing audible friction, we have the tongue movement that takes place in articulating the *high-front* vowel in *beat*. During the production of the vowel, the tongue shapes itself so as to throw the sound forward in the mouth; the vowel is therefore "advanced". A further raising of the front of the tongue would result in a consonant.

In like manner, for the *high-back* vowel in *boot*, the tongue is drawn back towards the soft palate, and, in the production of the sound, rises to the highest possible approach without causing audible friction while shaping itself so as to throw the sound back in the mouth, or "retract" it. The difference between these *high* vowels and what we may call the *high-drop* vowels in *bit* and *put* will be dealt with later.

Between the *high* vowels and the *low* vowels that will be considered directly, we have the various *mid* vowels, for which the tongue rises less than for the high vowels, and more than for the low ones. Thus, there are the front vowels heard in *wait, wet* and *where*, which we may call *high-mid, mid* and *low-mid*, respectively; and the back vowels heard in *boat* and *but*, which we may call *high-mid* and *low-mid*, respectively.

With least raising of the tongue, front and back, we produce the *low-front* vowel in *pat* and the *low-back* vowel in *part*. The two abnormally low and retracted vowels in the St. E. pronunciation of *caught* and *cot* may be named *low-drop-back* and *low-deep-back*, respectively. These have no parallel in the scheme of front vowels, as the lowest actual front vowel in English, viz. the sound in St. E. *pat*, requires a slight raising of the tongue towards the hard palate, with lowering of the jaw while this movement of the tongue takes place; without this tongue-movement the front of the tongue is too far from the hard palate to produce a front vowel, and the place of articulation is shifted to a central part (§ 90).

49. Vowel-sounds produced with both front and back of the tongue instrumental in forming them go by the name of "mixed" vowels. Thus, the vowel in *bird* is formed in St. E. by raising the central part of the tongue to low-mid, for which reason it is classed as *low-mid-mixed*. The central and mixed vowels will be dealt with after we have further considered the clearly front and back vowels.

In the table (§ 51) the vowels are classed as *high, mid,* or *low,* according to the extent to which the tongue rises while articulating them, and for the vowels in *caught* and *cot* according to the extent to which the tongue is lowered. It is a fallacy to assume that there are well-defined tongue positions for the normal vowel-sounds in St. E.

50. An old method of classification was to regard the vowels from the view-point of *close* and *open*. A close vowel, in the usual acceptation of the term, is one produced with relatively

narrow opening of the mouth, and an open vowel one produced with relatively wide opening of the mouth. But it only tends to confuse students if we adopt two different systems of classification for the vowels, and the terms *open* and *close* are at best vague and indefinite.

We will now proceed to tabulate the vowels in which front or back tongue-movement enables us to set up easily comprehensible distinctions between them, and assign to each vowel a definite symbol. As the Broad symbols are insufficient for this purpose, we must take a "narrower" notation, in order to avoid confusion. In this place it may be well to point out the chief differences between the Broad symbols given in § 16 and the Narrow symbols used in the following pages.

50.1. The length-mark ꞉ which is used with the Broad symbols to indicate the quality of a vowel-sound, as well as to show that the vowel in question is generally long or half-long, is only used with the Narrow symbols when the vowel is fully long, and has nothing to do with its quality; hence, ɑ꞉ appears as ɑ꞉ or ɑˑ, i꞉ as iꞏ or iˑ or even i, ɔ꞉ as ɔ꞉, ɔˑ or ɔ, u꞉ as u꞉ or uˑ, while ə꞉ is replaced by ɜ꞉ or ɜˑ.

This necessitates the use of special symbols in the Narrow transcript where the short vowel-symbols of the Broad transcript would be ambiguous; æ, ɛ and ʌ may be retained, as they can be supplied with the half-length mark without confusion, but i, u and ɔ must find substitutes: the adoption of ɪ and ʊ is explained in § 25; for ɔ we can use ɒ, and thus keep ɔˑ in *caught* distinct from the half-long ɒˑ in *cod*. The distinction between ə and ɜ is fully explained in § 85.

The Narrow symbols are therefore equally concerned with quality and length, to both of which the foreign student must

pay attention; he cannot be expected to know, for instance, that
the three i sounds in *reactively* (riːˈæktivli), as the word would
appear in the Broad form, are all different in quality; in the
Narrow form they appear as riˈæktɪvlɪ̆, the mark ˋ indicating
that the vowel has not so high a tongue-movement as the
normal ɪ (see § 73).

Though easier to interpret correctly than a Broad transcription, a Narrow one is harder to compose; but the difficulty of
using sufficiently accurate length-marks may be simplified in
the way shown in § 81.2.

The vowel-sounds analysed in the following paragraphs are
treated without any account being taken of the minute distinctions of sound set up by the position of a vowel in the
phonem (for "phonem" see Index of Subjects and Phonetic
Terms). After j or before r vowels are often shifted to a more
central position, while before liquids they are often slightly
lowered, as compared with their more usual method of formation. But distinctions of meaning do not depend upon such
sound-distinctions, which, in other words, are not significant.
They are produced mechanically by most speakers.

For the effect of l on vowels see § 117.

V

VOWEL-SOUNDS IN PRESENT-DAY STANDARD ENGLISH

51.   TABLE OF THE PRINCIPAL FRONT
AND BACK VOWELS.

Front		Back
i in *bead* (biːd)	high	u in *cooed* (kuːd)
ɪ in *bid* (bɪ·d)	high-drop	ʊ in *could* (kʊ·d)
ei in *bayed* (beid)	high-mid[1]	oᵘ in *code* (koᵘd)
ɛ in *bed* (bɛ·d)	mid	
ɛ̀ɜ in *bared* (bɛ̀ɜd)[2]	low-mid	ʌ in *cud* (kʌ·d)
æ in *bade* (bæ·d)	low	ɑ in *card* (kɑːd)
	low-drop	ɔ in *cord* (kɔːd)
	low-deep	ɒ in *cod* (kɒ·d)

¹ This refers to the main part of these two diphthongs; for the second element of them, when it is sounded, as in the key-words above, the tongue rises further to high-drop.

² The second element of this diphthong is a mixed vowel; see § 83.

52. In the keywords given above, the vowels marked fully long (ː), as well as the diphthongs eⁱ, ɛ̀ɜ and oᵘ—for which the length need not be indicated, as they are never short—are known as "long" vowels; those here marked half-long (·) are known as "short" vowels. The length of vowels is dealt with in detail in §§ 78, 81 and 135 *seq.* Here it may suffice to point out that all the vowels in the Table stand before a consonant that lengthens the vowel; before the corresponding voiceless consonant t the long vowels would be half-long, the short vowels quite short, i.e. half-long in *meat, mate, coot, coat, cart, caught,* and short in *bit, bet, bat, look, luck, lock.*

53. Rounded vowels, or those produced with more or less rounding of the lips, are u, ʊ, oᵘ and ɔ; the other vowels are unrounded. Tense vowels, relatively speaking, are i, u and ɔ; slightly tense are eⁱ, oᵘ and ɛɜ; in æ and ɒ there is slight pharyngeal tenseness only.

54. Mixed vowels are ə, as in the second syllable of *magazine*, and ɜ, as in the second syllable of *better*. The latter becomes a long vowel when stressed, as in *bird* (bɜːd), *hurt* (hɜˑt). Of these "murmur" vowels, ə is the neutral vowel, which occurs in many languages, whereas the ɜ in *better* is to all intents and purposes a shortened form of the vowel-sound in *bird*. The two sounds are dealt with fully in §§ 84–89.

Other diphthongs than those already mentioned are aɪ, as in *high*, aʊ, as in *house*, ɔɪ, as in *boy*, iɜ, as in *fear*, and ʊɜ, as in *poor*. These sounds are discussed in §§ 90–98.

We will now consider the principal vowels in detail.

BACK VOWELS

55. High-back, as in *boot, rude*. In forming this sound the mouth opens sufficiently wide to admit of the insertion of a thin lead-pencil; the lips are protruded and rounded; the muscles of the lips and cheeks are relatively tense, though not at the beginning of the sound, before the tongue has attained to the high position; the tongue is not left lying flat along the part that rises, but made convex or ridged. The main part of the vowel may therefore be described as high-back, retracted, tense, rounded. When fully long, uː, it is diphthongal in St. E. (see § 93); for length see § 81. After j or ç, as in *value* (**vælju**), *tune* (**tjuːn** or **tçuːn**), the vowel is less retracted (cf. § 83).

56. High-drop-back, as in *put, could*. The back of the tongue rises less than for u, and is flat instead of convex; the sound is

less retracted than u, i.e. it is "advanced"; the lip-rounding is diminished by half, while lips and cheeks are relaxed. This "lax" ʊ is generally short, occasionally half-long. There is also very slight lowering of the soft palate, but no resultant nasalizing. Description: high-drop-back, lax, advanced, slightly rounded.

57. High-mid-back, rising further to high-drop-back, as in *go, code*. For the first element of this oᵘ the mouth-opening is wider than for u, the lips are not so protruded, but should be rounded. In St. E. the sound is slightly tense when well articulated, and audibly diphthongal when not shortened, the little ᵘ of the oᵘ indicating a faint ʊ sound or an added rounding of the lips resembling w (see §§ 93, 94). The main part of the vowel in good speech is high-mid-back, advanced, tending to end in high-drop-back, slightly tense when long, and rounded.

58. In Northern E. the vowel is generally pure, oː or oˑ, i.e. is not diphthongal, and is tenser. In cockney speech the vowel has become something like **aow**, with no rounding till the **w** is reached.

59. The diphthongal nature of the St. E. oᵘ stands out most clearly when it is in a stressed syllable before a voiced consonant or finally, as in *load, intone, grow*. In longer words, or before a voiceless consonant in short words, as in *notable, token*, the diphthongal quality is often absent in good speech, and oˑ results. But the lip-rounding is always weak compared with that accompanying a typical continental o. When unrounded and advanced we have the very lax variety of this vowel, so prevalent to-day that it is imitated all too successfully by foreigners who have heard it frequently, much to the detriment of their English sounds. Even speakers of St. E. must constantly be on their guard against using an unrounded oː, and it would

seem as if the preservation of a carefully articulated o^u were threatened so seriously with being ousted from its precarious existence in St. E. speech, that we may soon have to deplore the fact that Englishmen whose speech-sounds are otherwise admirable cannot sound an o that resembles its continental relative. But it is not in England alone that slovenly articulation plays havoc with a melodious sound: in the dialect of Swedish spoken in Scania the o has become a sorry caterwaul— a caricature of an o—of which speakers of Standard Swedish make fun.

60. Low-mid-back, as in *but, bud, hull, mother*. This vowel is generally lax, short, unrounded, and with lips very slightly spread. The tongue, which is raised less than for o', is bunched somewhat in the centre, making the vowel difficult to analyse unless it is lengthened, and difficult to imitate. For foreign students the best approach to it is from the central-back a (see § 83), as in German *Hand*, French *palme*, by raising the tongue slightly higher than for a. Another way of getting to it is by aiming at a sound midway between ɑ and the œ in French *peur, seul*, but with spread lips and lax organs of articulation. An easy approach to it should be from its near neighbour, the vowel in *bird*, but this is a sound that gives many foreigners still more difficulty than ʌ. Theoretically viewed, the transition to ʌ should be made from its own ancestor, viz. ʊ, but the two sounds have diverged so widely in the course of time that they now produce quite different acoustic effects. But it need hardly be pointed out that ʊ remains the commonest substitute in the north of England and in Scotland for the St. E. sound in *but*. In the dialects ʌ is rare; other substitutes for it are a, ɑ and œ.

Note that ʌ for ʊ in some old-established pronunciations, e.g.

in *bull, bush, bosom, courier, butcher, cushion, full, pull, pulpit, push, put, sugar,* is regarded as provincial by speakers of St. E. It has been affirmed that in Northern E. there is an intermediate sound between ᴀ and ᴜ, viz. an unrounded ᴜ, but St. E. ᴜ can be sounded without lip-rounding and yet remain an entirely distinct sound from the ᴀ in *but,* which has become a comparatively low vowel-sound.

The spelling o in *mother, cover, constable* and many other words was introduced by the Norman French in positions where u proved to be an unsatisfactory symbol next to *v* (then written *u), n* or *m.* The spelling subsequently influenced the pronunciation, as in *accomplish, comrade, contrary, conduit* (kɒndɪt), *Brompton, Cromwell, Lombard, Covent Garden* (older *Convent G.*), etc. In some words two pronunciations are still struggling for the upper hand: *frontier,* which was frɒntiə until the present century was well fledged, is now frᴀntiə or frᴀntjə, *dromedary* has become drɒmɪdərɪ rather than drᴀmɪdərɪ, but proper names, such as *Ponsonby, Coverley,* remain unaffected by spelling-pronunciations.

61. Low-back, as in *card, cart.* Mouth-opening fairly wide, no rounding, lips and cheeks lax, but some pharyngeal tenseness is needed to prevent the vowel from being advanced, which is still the dialect variety of it in the majority of cases. The vowel has become a clear and sonorous phone in St. E., and is supplanting the older a and intermediate sounds between a and ɑː to an ever greater extent. There was a time when this open, clear ɑː was regarded as a vulgarity, and "refined" speakers carefully avoided it; but during the last half-century or so ɑː has supplanted a and the intermediate sound between a and ɑː in many words, while in others it has won ground at the expense of æ, and any impression of affectation in the pronunciation

of *glass* as glɑːs is no longer produced on educated speakers of English in any of its British varieties.

62. Note that in the pronunciation of ɑː the middle of the tongue rises in proportion to the lowering of the jaw, evidently to compensate for the enlargement of the mouth-cavity (see Grandgent, *Vowel Measurements*, 1890). Some phoneticians have classed ɑ as a mixed vowel, because the back of the tongue is not absolutely so high as the front; but it is at the back that the tongue comes nearest to the palate, so that the place of greatest constriction is back (see Jespersen, *Articulations of Speech Sounds*).

63. Foreign speakers, from whom one might expect to hear a resonant back vowel, show an increasing tendency in some countries, notably Italy, to substitute for it an advanced, even palatal, vowel. The cockney, on the other hand, throws the sound too far back in the mouth, making it like an unrounded ɔ; symbol *A*. The same tendency is observable in Low German, and in parts of Sweden—Västergötland and Bohuslän (see § 206).

64. Low-drop-back, as in *bought, caught, cord*. This is a lowered, retracted variety of ɑː, with considerable lip-rounding and tenseness. One of its characteristic features is its length. Symbol ɔː or ɔˑ. An older form of it is ɔˑɜ, still current in American speech, and in English dialects. Description: low-drop-back, tense, rounded.

65. A short, lax, and considerably higher variety of ɔ is the first element of the diphthong in *boy, noise* (see further, §§ 73 and 92).

66. In St. E. the vowel-sounds in *sought* and *sort* are now absolutely identical, two different sounds having been levelled under one form. But as the dialects still preserve a distinction between them it is not permissible in poetry to rime together

such words as *law* and *bore*, for it is only in St. E. that they are true rimes. On the other hand, vowels that were once identical but have diverged since, e.g. *floor* and *poor*, are still allowable rimes.

67. Low-deep-back, as in *cod*, *cot*. The back of the tongue is abnormally lowered in articulating the St. E. variety of this vowel,[1] there is hardly any rounding of the lips, which, together with the cheeks, are lax; but there is slight tenseness in the throat. The description is therefore: low-deep-back, lax, though with slight pharyngeal tenseness, unrounded.

68. For the typical St. E. low-deep-back vowel, symbol ɒ, the tongue is lowered so much at the back that this is a difficult sound for speakers to acquire who do not possess it in their own language. They naturally substitute for it a higher vowel-sound. Thus, Danes regularly replace it by a sound closely resembling the St. E. ʌ in *but* (see § 60). A similar substitute is made by many educated speakers of Northern and Western E., their vowel-sound being made with the tongue rising higher at the back than for ɑː; with such speakers the whisper-pitch of ɒ can be actually higher than that of ɔː. In America, ɑ regularly supplants ɒ in good speech, and may be regarded as the St. American form of it.

The process of lengthening the St. E. ɒ, as in *cod*, imposes a strain on the throat, which can be distinctly felt when the throat is in an inflamed condition. This may account for the fact that ɒ is scarcely ever fully lengthened. In common with other "short" vowels it becomes half-long before an unsupported

[1] Jespersen (*Modern English Grammar*, Part I, Ch. xv) says of ɒ, "back of the tongue very much lowered"; of ɔː, "back of the tongue not quite so much lowered as for ɒ"; of ɑː, "back of the tongue raised a little towards the soft palate". Sweet, in his *Sounds of English* (1908), still classed ɑː as low-mid; but see § 101.

voiced consonant other than a liquid, as in *dog* (dɒ·g). To substitute dɔːg for dɒ·g, or gɔːd for gɒ·d, is a vulgarism in modern speech.

69. This lengthened ɒ· must not be confounded with the half-long ɔ· that is used by many speakers of St. E. in *cross, cost, cough, off, often, loft, soften, salt* and a few other words. In these a fully long ɔː is no longer heard in Standard speech, and a short ɒ, though with a higher tongue-movement than for St. E. ɒ, is typically Northern E. The tendency in recent times among speakers of St. E. to shorten the vowel in these words has been attributed by some phoneticians to the influence of the Northern forms, but it is more probably another example of the constantly shifting vowel-lengths that have characterized English vowels in the course of their history. If St. E. had kept the long vowel-sounds in these words, the provinces would have followed suit as soon as speakers in influential circles had set the fashion. In American speech the long ɔː has lived on in these instances with conservative fidelity, the minority that shorten the vowel-sound pronouncing it as ɑ.

The St. E. form krɔ·s for *cross* is thus represented in American speech by either krɔːs or krɑs. For St. E. ɒ, American speech has either ɑ, as in *stop*, or ɔ, as in *dog*. Pronunciations with low-deep ɒ are rare.

FRONT VOWELS

70. In these the front of the tongue is chiefly instrumental in giving the vowels their quality. In St. E. the front vowel for which the tongue rises highest is the vowel in *bead*, the vowel with the least raising of the tongue the one in *bat*. The sequence from high to low is less clearly differentiated than in the case of the back vowels, there being less scope for modi-

fying the resonance chamber; the mobility of the front of the tongue compared with the back is more than counterbalanced by the mobility of the soft palate as against the immobility of the hard.

71. High-front, as in *bead* (biːd), *beat* (biˑt), *re-enter* (riˈɛntə), *let me see* (lɛt mi siː). The lips are spread outwards, the tongue is relatively tense, though the tenseness does not begin at once; like uː the vowel is of a diphthongal nature, unless it is short. The tongue rises convexedly as it grows tenser, and ends by being almost high enough for articulating j (see § 93). The main part of the vowel is high-front, tense, unrounded.

72. High-drop-front, as in *bid* (bɪˑd), *bit* (bɪt). The tongue does not rise so high as for i, is not advanced, and is flattened; lips and cheeks are unrounded, and the muscles of the tongue are lax. The shift in the place of articulation from i to ɪ is similar to that of u to ʊ, though here it is retracted instead of advanced, and the difference between high and high-drop greater than in the case of the back vowel: ɪ compared with iː is considerably retracted. Description: high-drop-front retracted, lax, unrounded. There is frequently slight lowering of the soft palate, but without any nasal effect.[1]

Before a liquid in an unstressed syllable, ɪ tends to disappear after sibilants, as in *pencil, fossil, messenger*.

When followed by another vowel in an unstressed syllable, as in *cordial, meridian, various, twentieth*, we have a closer and advanced vowel, which becomes j in quick speech, kɔːdɪəl becoming kɔːdjəl.[2]

[1] Professor Jones calls my attention to a curious tendency Americans have of diphthongizing ɪ, so that *bid* becomes bɪᵊd.

[2] This j is an example of a semi-vowel, being a sound that differs from a true consonant in that it lacks the frictional element which is characteristic of normal fricative consonants, such as f, v, s, z. It might also

73. Another vowel-sound, common in St. E., and one that many foreign students find difficult to imitate, is the extra-lax variety of ɪ, or a vowel in which the tongue only rises to high-mid. Symbol ɩ. It is very common finally, as in *merry, city*, but also occurs in other unstressed syllables, as in *palace, language, accurate, portrait, captain*. It is very frequent when the nomic spelling has *e*, especially in inflected forms such as *horses, added,* and is used by many speakers of St. E. for ə in the endings *-less* and *-ness*, as in *careless, business*. Historically, ɩ is here probably older than ə.[1]

Note that the substitution of ɪ for ɩ in *cruel, fuel, Margate* and many other words is a distinct cockneyism; to rime *scarlet* with *starlit* is pure cockney.[2] Some words have never submitted to this sound-change: *claret* remains klærət, *asset*, æsɛt.

ɩ is also the second element in the diphthong ɔɪ, as the tongue does not rise to more than high-mid, but the exact symbol is not called for here, since the distance the tongue has to travel to get from the raised ɔ in this diphthong—about low-mid-back—across to the ɪ element, induces it to fall short in the raising of the tongue, and a mid-front or even mixed vowel results. But elsewhere ɩ serves a useful purpose by accentuating differences obscured by the Broad symbols. Thus, the trio siːt, sit, siti convey no warning to the beginner who is likely to

be classed as a vowel-glide. On the other hand, the voiceless consonant corresponding to j, viz. ç, which may be heard in many speakers' pronunciation of the initial sound in *huge* and a few other words, is a true fricative (see § 112). The other semi-vowel in St. E. is the voiced w, in which the organs of articulation assume the position for sounding uː, but pass over to the position required for articulating the vowel that follows (see § 197). The voiceless variety of w, which does not exist in St. E., is a true fricative consonant (see § 111).

[1] Communicated by Professor Otto Jespersen.
[2] All Londoners are apt to do this.

mispronounce both ɪ and ì, whereas siːt, sɪt, sɪtì give him the
necessary danger-signals.

74. High-mid-front advanced is the extent the tongue rises
for the first element of the diphthong heard in the St. E.
pronunciation of *rain, fade, bay*. Tongue and lips are slightly
tense, lips unrounded. For the second element the tongue rises
further to high-drop-front. Symbol eⁱ. The e of this eⁱ is not so
high or tense as the continental e, as in French *été*, and if
greater exactitude were required it could be transcribed èⁱ. For
Northern E. see § 26. In St. E. the diphthongal quality of the
vowel is heard when the vowel is final or when stressed before
a voiced consonant; otherwise the diphthongal quality is
obscured or entirely lacking, as in *laity* (leˑɪtì), *lately, mistaken*.

75. Mid-front, as in *let, bed*. Tongue and lips relaxed, lips
unrounded; tongue does not rise quite so high for this vowel as
for the e in *late*, and the sound is more retracted. Symbol ɛ.

As many foreigners have difficulty in making the requisite
distinction between the vowels in *pen* and *pain* (pɛn), (peⁱn),
fez and *phase* (fɛˑz), (feⁱz), *debt* and *date* (dɛt), (deⁱt), the symbol ɛ
helps to accentuate the difference. In length ɛ is either quite
short, as in *bet*, or half-long, as in *bed* (bɛˑd). Frenchmen are
prone to lengthen it in any position, and substitute for it a
tense vowel é. In Northern E. the tongue does not rise higher
than for the first element in the St. E. diphthong heard in
bare (see § 76).

76. Between the mid-front ɛ in *bed* and the low-front æ in *bad*
comes the first element of the diphthong heard in *bear, rare,
hair, Aaron*. For this, if we must speak of the element *per se*,
we can employ the symbol è, the grave accent indicating that
the sound is a trifle lower than the ɛ in St. E. *bed*. If we require
a name for it we can call it low-mid-front, which is justified by

the relation in which it stands to the mixed vowel in *bird* and the back vowel in *bud* (cf. Diagram, p. 47). But since this ɛ̀ is always followed in St. E. by a murmur, we can omit the modifier when dealing with the diphthong *per se*, as the employment of the same symbol for the vowel in *bed* and the first element of the diphthong in *bared* can lead to no confusion.

77. The murmur vowel in this diphthong is either ə or ɜ, sounds discussed in §§ 84–89; the ə murmur only comes before intervocal r, as in *fairy* (fɛərì); otherwise it takes the form ɜ, as in *fair* (fɛɜ), *fairly* (fɛɜlì). In St. E. ɛə and ɛɜ are diphthongs consisting of a low-mid-front vowel followed by a murmur, the first element being very slightly tense and unrounded. The diphthong is never short, but the brunt of the length falls on the first element when followed by ə, and is borne by both when the second element is ɜ (see § 88). When this ɜ is final, or stands before a single voiced consonant, as in *care*, *cared*, the second element has the greater length. In this last case, shortening of the second element is characteristic of the speech of Indians, and of the negroes of North America.

78. Low-front, as in *bat*, *bad*. Symbol æ. For formation, see § 48. In sounding this vowel the mouth opens wider than for any other vowel in St. E.; lips and cheeks are unrounded and lax, but there is tenseness pharyngeally, which keeps the soft palate from being lowered. This makes æ a troublesome vowel to sing, and singers generally substitute for it the vowel a (see § 90), on which a long note can be sustained without straining the throat.

As regards length, æ is quite anomalous. Though classed as short in the older books that touch on English pronunciation, it can assume any length. Even when shortest, i.e. before the voiceless plosives (see § 81.2), it is longer than any other "short" vowel; it is at least half-long before nasals and the voiceless fricatives (cf. the Tables in § 81.2), as in *gas, cash, man*; it is long in other cases, as in *fag, cab, pad*, and over-long in the adjectives *bad, glad, mad, sad* when used predicatively, the length being very effective in Browning's well-known lines

> How sad and bad and mad it was—
> But then, how it was sweet!

When æ is short it is more retracted than when long; in this particular, again, it partakes of the nature of both short and long vowels. In a word, æ is a compromise between long and short vowels.

79. Norwegians and many Germans have difficulty in sounding a clear æ; they do not lower the jaw enough, and shorten the vowel, so that they produce a vowel resembling ε. Such speakers make no acoustic difference between *man* and *men*, *dad* and *dead*, *Alice* and *Ellis*, *Annie* and *any*, etc. The fault can generally be cured by insisting on a wider mouth-opening for æ. Frenchmen, on the other hand, are inclined to retract the æ from a front to a central one, making it resemble the Northern E. a; in Parisian speech, however, as in *patte*, the a is almost as much advanced as the St. E. æ. The cockney substitute of ε for æ seems to be losing ground rapidly.

80. The scale of front vowels in St. E. from low to high is thus represented in the words *lad, laird, led, laid, lid, lead*, or in *marry, Mary, merry, maid, mid, mead*. Note that as the tongue rises higher the lips accompany the movement by spreading outwards. Tenseness in front vowels in St. E. is merely relative where it exists, not absolute; compared with the really tense vowels in French or Swedish, they might even be classed in a lump as lax.

A PRELIMINARY NOTE ON THE LENGTH OF
VOWEL-SOUNDS IN STANDARD ENGLISH

81. It will have been gathered from what has been stated above that tenseness is generally associated in St. E. with length, that long vowels lose in length before voiceless consonants, and that short vowels gain in length before voiced consonants other than liquids; but that æ disassociates itself from the short vowels in assuming length before liquids. The question naturally arises: to what extent do short vowels gain in length when lengthened, and how do they compare with long vowels that have been shortened?

81.1. As the ear cannot make sufficiently fine distinctions, we must have recourse to experimental phonetics. Kymograph records of my own pronunciation show that the average length of the vowel in *hid* (hɪ·d) is 24½ hundredths of a second, that in *heat* (hi·t) just over 20. The two vowels are thus approximately of the same length, and the transcribed forms true to the facts. But with the broad forms hid and hiːt the facts are not only obscured but distorted, since they suggest that the vowels are alike in quality but differ in length—the very opposite of the truth. The foreign student who makes the vowel in *hid* appreciably shorter than the vowel in *heat* must therefore look to his pronunciation in this important particular; he may find that the underlying principles in English run counter to those that obtain in his own language.

81.2. How formidable a task it is to lay down hard and fast rules for the length of English vowel-sounds may be deduced from the results obtained from short, stressed words, even if we restrict our enquiry to vowels that stand in a final position or are followed by a single consonant.

As it is only the long vowels that occur in a final position, we get this result for short vowels:

Short vowels are (1) shortest before voiceless plosives[1] and 1; (2) next shortest before nasals and voiceless fricatives;[2] (3) longest before other voiced consonants (see § 110).

But as, under similar conditions, high vowels are shorter than low ones, and æ is longer than the others, we can group the results in the three classes, from shortest to longest, as in this Table:

I	II	III
pit, put, fill, pull	wish, dim, push	could, bid
pet, dwell	guess, men	bed, bud
cot	bus, come, song	cod
pat, cap	cash, gas, man	fag, cab, pad

In class I the vowels from *pit* to *cot* range from $13\frac{1}{2}$ to 20 hundredths of a second; æ averages $22\frac{1}{2}$. In class II the lengths from *wish* to *song* range from $17\frac{1}{2}$ to 24; æ averages 29. In class III the lengths from *could* to *cod* range from $21\frac{1}{2}$ to 31; æ averages $35\frac{1}{2}$.

It is thus in classes II and III that æ differs most markedly from the other short vowels: if we compare the vowels in *men* and *man* we find the former has a length of 21, the latter 29; in class III the average of the other short vowels is 25, of æ $35\frac{1}{2}$.

In short, stressed words the long vowels and diphthongs before single consonant-sounds or when final show the following results:

(1) Shortest before voiceless plosives; (2) next shortest before voiceless fricatives and 1; (3) next longest before nasals or when final; (4) longest before other voiced consonants.

---

[1] I.e. p, t, tʃ and k.   [2] I.e. f, θ, s and ʃ.

The following Table shows how short vowels (cols. 1–3),
æ (col. 4), and long vowels (cols. 5–8), compare in length; the
range of length in each class is shown by the figures on the left
of the Table:

	1	2	3	4	5	6	7	8
13								
	pit foot duck	pull fill						
17								
	fop	wish, dim push, men bun	nib should		peep boot	deal		
22								
		buss loss upon guess	bid bud fizz	pat shall	coat, cape pipe about	goose sail, piece fall, pace	see(n)	
28								
			buzz says bed cod	gas man has	curt fork	purse, louse force	boon pain turn term	leave shooed
33								
				fag		path wife	tome town thorn toe mine cow	nose, nave bared beard card board bowed
43								

The above are from copious kymograph records of my pronunciation taken and measured by Dr E. A. Meyer. For
further examples, see §§ 135, 136.

As it would complicate the marking of vowel-length if we
adhered to the results to be derived from the above Table,
which show the vowels in *nib* and *should* to be as long as the
vowels in *peep* and *boot*, or the vowel in *deal* to be shorter than
the vowel in *bid, bud, fizz, says, buzz, bed* and *cod*, it will simplify

matters if we mark all the short vowels in col. 3 as half-long, and all the vowels in cols. 5 and 6 as half-long, keeping full-length marks for the fully long æ, lowest compartment of col. 4, as well as for all the vowels of cols. 7 and 8. This simplification is moreover justified by the faculty long vowels have of retaining some of their length in connected speech.

Foreign students should make a note of the short and long vowels in compartment 22–28, for they frequently make the vowels in *bid* (brˑd), *bud* (bʌˑd), *fizz* (frˑz) too short, and the vowels in *goose* (guˑs), *piece* (piˑs) too long; so also with the vowels in compartment 28–33, with the half-long vowels in *bed* (bɛˑd), *cod* (kɒˑd), *force* (fɔˑs). Half-length should be aimed at in all such cases, and the half-length mark utilized.

81.3. Before two consonants, vowels generally lose in length compared with the lengths noted above. For the short vowels, see §§ 138–141. With long vowels this is most noticeable when the vowel is followed by a nasal supported by a voiceless consonant: cf. *darn* (dɑːn) with *dance* (dɑˑns), *learn* (lɜːn) with *learnt* (lɜˑnt), *nine* (naɪn) with *ninth*. See moreover § 136.

81.4. In words of two syllables, the first of which consists of a short unstressed prefix, the above rules hold good: *disease* (dɪˈziːz), etc.

Otherwise, in words of two syllables vowels lose considerably in length, the short vowels that averaged from 13–22 in the Table being reduced to 6½–16½ in col. 1, those in col. 3 that averaged from 17–33 being reduced to 11–18; in other words, all short vowels, even including æ, become short. Of the long vowels, the high ones become short, the others half-long, with the vowels ɑ and ɔ, and the diphthongs aɪ and aʊ, retaining greater length than the rest—that is to say, as far as conclusions can be drawn from the material examined. Generally speaking, we may say that in words of two or more syllables stressed vowels lose in length, most noticeably the short vowels that are half-long in short words: cf. *cab* (**kæ·b** or **kæːb**) with *cabby* (**kæbi**). In unstressed words there is, almost invariably, considerable loss of length. But a vast amount of spade-work still remains to be done in this domain before the facts can be sifted and set out in detail.

Here it may suffice to draw attention to the rule that long vowels and diphthongs lose in length when they are immediately followed by an unstressed vowel in the same word, e.g. *seeing* (**si·ıŋ**), *laity* (**le·ıti**), *poetry* (**po·ıtri**), *stoic* (**sto·ık**).

81.5. A factor which undoubtedly influences length in vowels, as well as in consonants, is the emotional quality of words, or some emotion on the part of the speaker. Without attempting to delve in this tempting field, we may assume that the emotional concomitance causes the vowel to be long or over-long in the adjective *bad*, but leaves it half-long in the past tense *bade* (**bæ·d**) from *bid*. Or again, a very emphatic *was* may be pronounced with a fully long vowel, as in "So he *was*". Words of a poetic or religious type are frequently pronounced with an extra-long vowel, as in *abide*. The degree of emotion behind the word may explain the inconstant length of such common words as *yes* and *well*, the vowel in the former being often made fully long or over-long, while in the latter the lengthening may affect either the vowel or the final consonant, or even both.

For vowels in unstressed syllables see also §§ 142, 143.

THE VOWEL TRIANGLE

82. In the preface to his *Handbook of Phonetics* (1877) Henry Sweet wrote: "The confusion is made worse by the assumption that all vowel sounds must necessarily fit in as intermediates

between the supposed primitive vowels *a*, *i* and *u*, whence that unfortunate triangular arrangement of the vowels which has done so much to perpetuate error and prevent progress". The arrangement in question is one that shows back and front vowels becoming less widely differentiated in the series from high to low, until they meet at a point which marks the apex of an inverted triangle. The triangle looks so simple and practical that it has outlived Dr Sweet's warning by over half a century, in part no doubt because it has endeared itself to all who admire a perfectly symmetrical figure. But the fact remains that the diagram is only so symmetrical because the vowels are made to conform, willy-nilly, with the lines forming the two sides of the triangle. For all the front vowels to end exactly on one of the two converging lines, they would have to become uniformly less advanced from high to low; and for the back vowels to be equally accommodating they would have to become uniformly less retracted as the tongue-movement differed for their formation. A language, if such a one existed, in which this phenomenon occurred, would be ideal in that one respect, though it might be impossible to master by anyone save a native; in any case, the attempt to adhere rigidly to the triangle scheme for the English vowels is quite unfeasible.

The plan of showing how back and front vowels actually do approximate as they become lower may, however, be attempted by indicating roughly the differences in tongue-movement from high to low vowels by marking the point reached by the tongue for each vowel along or within converging lines, and abandoning any attempt to induce them to meet at an apex. The resultant figure, as based on an analysis of my own vowel-sounds, has little resemblance to a triangle; it is rather like a truncated cone with an appendix trailing away from the converging lines and completing the work of ruining any attempt at symmetry. Nevertheless, it may prove useful in helping to illustrate what has already been said about the vowels in St. E., and what remains to be said in the sections that follow.

For an explanation of the symbols a and ù, of the dotted lines, and of the term "central", see § 83. The symbol ɛ̀ stands for the first element in the word *air* (ɛɜ); ì is the final sound in *any*; ɜ is used for the stressed or unstressed vowel in *murmur*, and ə for the neutral vowel in the first syllable of *about, upon, connect,* or in the second syllable of *canvas, jealous, stirrup.* For the other symbols see the keywords below the Diagram.

The tongue-movement for the first element in o^u, as in *code*, is given as reaching a more retracted position than is to be heard in the cockneyfied sound so prevalent in London at the present time—say, 1930—but I need hardly apologize for having a vowel that differs somewhat from that uglification; cf. moreover § 59.

NOTES ON THE DIAGRAM

83. The connecting link between back and front vowels is seen to be a vowel, intermediate between St. E. æ and ɑ, which may be articulated either immediately in front of the central point of the tongue, or immediately back of the central point. The former variety of a is heard in the usual form of the Northern E. substitute for æ, as in *bad*. We may call this the central-front a, a sound almost identical with the non-Parisian *a* in *patte*. In Parisian French the sound is advanced towards æ. Compared with these varieties of a, the German short *a* in *man* is a central-back vowel, i.e. a sound retracted towards ɑ.

Compared with St. E. ɑ, the Parisian ɑ in *pas* is lower, i.e. it is low-drop-back, not low-back, and would therefore find its

DIAGRAM SHOWING CONNECTION BETWEEN
VOWELS IN STANDARD SPEECH

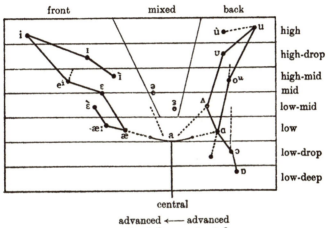

central

advanced ⟵— advanced
retracted —⟶ retracted

Keywords

bead   cue cooed
        bid   could
   bayed   forty   code
        bed   upon
        bared   murmur   cud
          bad bat   **a**   card
                                      cord
                                        cod

For **a** see § 83.

place in the Diagram at the end of the dotted line that continues the line from o^u to ɑ. On the other hand, the French ɔ in *corde* is a low-mid-back, not a low-drop-back, vowel. It would therefore find its place at the end of the dotted line that rises from ɔ. Similarly the ɔ in Northern E.

Compared with the central-back a, the ʌ in *but* is raised from low to low-mid, a very slight difference in reality. If this ʌ be somewhat advanced it is brought into the mixed tongue position, the one for articulating the ɜ in *bird* (bɜːd). This sound, raised and slightly advanced, gives us the neutral vowel heard in the unstressed syllables of *upon, stirrup*. Foreign students can generally reproduce this last, the ə, without difficulty, but it is not advisable to make comparisons that start from such a weakly articulated phone as this. Moreover, the German ə in *Gabe* is a more advanced vowel than the English one, many German speakers using a sound here that is very nearly the same sound as English ɛ in *get*.

The positions given for e^i and o^u indicate the points of departure for these diphthongs. The diphthong aɪ starts a little above the central-front a position, and rises to ɪ; the diphthong aʊ starts between central-back a and ʌ, rising almost to ʊ.

With regard to the much discussed quality of the vowel-sound marked u̇, which is the vowel heard in St. E. when u is preceded by the palatal fricative j or ç, as in *value* (vælju), *tune* (tjuːn or tçuːn), the u is advanced and lax; but as the whisper-pitch of this advanced u does not, in my pronunciation at least, differ essentially from the vowel in *root*, either in an accented or an unaccented syllable, the symbol u̇ need only be used for purposes of comparison.

St. E. æ, ʌ and ɔ have no counterpart in St. Swedish, whereas the ɒ in St. E. *rock* is almost identical with the *o* in Swedish *rock*, though the latter lacks pharyngeal tenseness. The Danish *a* in *ja* is closely reminiscent of St. E. æ. There is also a marked similarity between the diphthongs in St. E. *high, house, boy* and the Swedish vowels in the words *haj, paus, boj*.

MIXED VOWELS

Far less easy to analyse than the front or back vowels are the vowels known as "mixed" (see § 49). We have already (§ 62) stated the reason for classing ɑː as a back vowel. In dialects and in the speech of many Americans the vowel ʌ is often a mixed vowel, approximating to the vowel-sound in *bird*; the sound is advanced in that case.

84. In St. E. the mixed vowels are the two forms of the vocal murmur. One of these, the neutral vowel, for which the Broad and Narrow symbol is ə, is heard in the unstressed syllables of the words *about, aloud, upon, connect, canvas, jealous, stirrup*. This murmur is always quite short, and only occurs in unstressed syllables; it is sometimes reduced to a mere whisper, as in *pathetic* (pəθetɪk); it never comes at the end of a breath-group, i.e. a group of sounds articulated without a pause (§ 176). It takes the place of vowels that have lost all their original quality and have become quite characterless. It presents no difficulty to most foreign speakers. It often serves as a featureless supporting vowel between consonant-sounds, as in *seldom* (seldəm). Description: mid-mixed, front of tongue rising slightly higher than for ɜ, lax, unrounded.

85. Far more resonant is the murmur in the unstressed syllables of *doctor, ever, figure*. When lengthened it is the vowel in *stern, hurl, work, bird*. Symbol ɜ. This vowel is very common in terminations, occurs very frequently at the end of a breath-group, and may be any length. It is quite long in *stern* (stɜːn),

half-long in *offered*, and short in *eagerly* (iːgₐlĭ). In the vast majority of cases ₃ has developed from a vowel that is followed in the nomic script by the letter *r*;[1] it has a more sonorous quality than ₐ, is slightly lower and very nearly a back vowel. Description: low-mid-mixed, tense when long, unrounded.[2]

For the fully long, tense sound the tongue is somewhat hollowed in front. In dialects, as in American E., ₃—but never ₐ—is sounded with the blade of the tongue drawn back; the result is a coronal or cacuminal vowel, symbol ʒ. But before the intervocal **r** of derivatives the coronal quality generally disappears.

86. The ₃ murmur causes foreign students infinite trouble, it being a new vowel to the majority of them. Their inability to reproduce it correctly is clearly revealed when the vowel is long: they are wont to substitute for it a rounded vowel like

---

[1] Final *-a* in *sofa, vanilla, Asia*, etc., *-ah* in *verandah, Sarah*, etc. have in St. E. practically fallen into line with words ending in *-ar, -er, -or* and *-ur*, though purists and elocutionists still attempt to keep a sound here that more closely resembles ɑː. See also § 128.

[2] The broad symbol for ₃, i.e. ₐ when short or half-long, ₐː when long, thus apparently identifying ₃ with the neutral vowel described in § 84, gives rise to great confusion. In the first place, the neutral vowel in *about, upon* is always quite short in English speech; to use the symbol ₐ for it is perfectly satisfactory; but the employment of the same symbol with a length-mark affixed to it in order to represent a vowel-sound that differs acoustically from it, as in *sir, bird*, is a dangerous device, because the vowel ₐ when lengthened does not assume the quality of the vowel-sound in *bird*, any more than the vowel in *cud* can become the vowel-sound in *card* when lengthened, or the vowel in *cod* assume the quality of the vowel in *cord* (cf. *cod* (kɒˑd) and *caught* (kɔˑt), where the two vowels have approximately the same length). Moreover, the vowel-sound in *bird* may be shortened, as in *offered* (ɒfₐˑd), *hours* (auₐˑz), or become quite short, as in the second syllable of *eagerly, energy*. Two distinct symbols are thus required, one for the neutral vowel in *about* (ₐbaut), *upon* (ₐpɒn), another for the typically English murmur in *refer* (rĭˈfₐː), *eagerly* (iːgₐlĭ), *differs* (dĭfₐˑz). See, furthermore, the note to § 89.

the one in French *peuple* or German *können*, followed by a faint uvular *r*, i.e. ʀ. Thus, for bɜːd they say bœᴿd. As long as they persist in rounding the sound they will mispronounce the English ɜ; and note that the rounding that they employ is not lip-rounding—which would not matter much—but inner rounding, with narrowing between the back of the tongue and the uvula. Spreading the lips may help to counteract this fault, but with some speakers, Germans especially, it seems an almost insuperable task to get them to eliminate the rounding altogether. Yet until they do so they will fail to produce the typically English vowel in *bird*. They must remember, too, that any attempt to indicate the presence of the *r* that has been absorbed by the vowel-sound results in a phone that is unknown to St. E.

87. The difference between ə and ɜ can be brought out by comparing such pairs as *formally* and *formerly*, *seven* and *Severn*, *Oban* and *Cockburn* (koᵘbɜn), *Weston* and *western*. Pronunciations such as sʌbəb for sʌbɜb (*suburb*), ɛkspət for ɛkspɜt (*expert*), ɛnədʒɪ for ɛnɜdʒɪ (*energy*), pætən for pætɜn (*pattern*), slʌgəd for slʌgɜd (*sluggard*), are careless or slipshod. The opposite fault—substitution of ɜ for ə—occurs when an emphatical speaker says *symperthy* (sɪmpɜθɪ) for sɪmpəθɪ, or the cockney *ternight* (tɜnaɪt) for tənaɪt.

As ə does not occur finally in connected speech in English, while ɜ is common in such a position, an Englishman has great difficulty in using ə finally; but he must learn to do so in speaking foreign languages, or he will make countless mistakes. Thus, he will pronounce the German word *Wunde*, "wound", vʊndə, as vʊndɜ, which latter[1] can only represent *Wunder*, "wonder".

---

[1] The German ɜ vowel is produced with pharyngeal tenseness.

88. In unstressed syllables the ɜ murmur, like any other
vowel, can be so indistinctly articulated that its quality is quite
obscured, and it is then indistinguishable from ə. Thus, *persistent* (pɜˈsɪstənt) is turned into pəˈsɪstənt; but careful speakers
avoid these clipped forms, as well as the drawled or over-
emphatic pɜːˈsɪstənt. If the ɜ of the prefix is properly articulated,
it is neither the neutral ə, nor the vowel ɜ lengthened. What
matters is the quality of the vowel, much more than the length,
which may be left to look after itself. When, in *The Merchant of
Venice*, Shylock says: "Are there balances here to weigh the
flesh?", how is the word *there* to be adequately transcribed?
The transcription ðə cannot stand, as it would be interpreted
as *the*; nor will ðɛə do, since it might be taken to mean *their*;
the form ðɜ is free from ambiguity.[1]

When final, unstressed ɜ is never quite short, but since it has
this slight lengthening in common with any unstressed vowel
at the end of a breath-group, it need not be marked in the
transcript. But the length may well be indicated when unstressed ɜ is followed by a voiced consonant, as in *uttered* (ʌtɜ·d),
hours (aʊɜ·z), *appears* (əpiɜ·z).

The ɜ forming part of, or following, a diphthong is weakened
to ə before the sounded r of derivatives: *air* (ɛɜ) but *airy* (ɛərɪ),
near but *nearer* (niərɜ),[2] *Ireland* (aɪɜlənd) but *Irish* (aɪərɪʃ) (see
also § 124). Otherwise the ɜ retains its quality before the r of
derivatives, as in *ogreish* (oᵘgɜrɪʃ) from *ogre* (oᵘgɜ). It also
persists in compounds such as *ear-ring* (iɜrɪŋ).[3]

---

[1] In this connection I take it that Dickens was committing a very
intentional *blunder* in *David Copperfield* when he turned *Blundestone*
(blʌndəstən), Suffolk, into *Blunderstone* (blʌndɜstən); Dickens had a very
keen ear for sound-effects.

[2] Americans say nɪɜ, but nɪˈrɜ.

[3] Cf. *ear-ring* (iɜrɪŋ) with *earing* (iərɪŋ), "a small line to fasten a reef-
band; the formation of ears, as in wheat".

89. Some phoneticians who employ the narrow transcription of the I.P.A. have adopted ɜ for the stressed vowel in *murmur*, but have retained the broad symbol ə for the unstressed vowel. This is likely to confuse foreign students. If ɜ be used, with the required length-mark, for the stressed vowel in *murmur*, it had better be used for the unstressed vowel as well, since the two vowels possess much the same quality, though differing in length. To distinguish the quality of the one from that of the other would mean making hair-splitting distinctions that could serve no useful purpose. On the other hand, the employment of ə alone for both the neutral vowel and the typically English vocal murmur invests it with far too wide a scope; but it would seem that this symbol, having already been overworked so long, is to go on being overworked till doomsday.[1]

[1] The danger of overworking ə can be exemplified from that indispensable reference work, Daniel Jones's *Pronouncing Dictionary*, which employs a broad notation. There we find *lion* transcribed laiən and *iron*, aiən, which would justify a foreigner in concluding that *lion* and *iron* were good rimes in St. E.; they are nothing of the kind. Again, for *suppose* we are given səpouz or spouz, but for *surprise* only one form, səpraiz. But why this invidious distinction? The combination spr is no more difficult for an English tongue to articulate than the combination sp: there are at least a hundred words in the English language beginning with *spr*-! The solution of the mystery is simply that the murmurs in *suppose* and *surprise* are of a different quality, the former being a less sonorous phone, which can be reduced to a whisper, or disappear altogether, in rapid speech, whereas the latter persists owing to its greater sonority.

The trouble with the broad symbols is that they are often ambiguous, as the above examples show. Foreigners using this dictionary discover to their embarrassment that the same symbol may stand for two, or even three, different sounds. In his *English Phonetics* Professor Jones gives ten principal rules that must be remembered by those interpreting a broad transcription; but, apart from the fact that the ten rules do not even cover the cases pointed out above, it is too much to expect of a foreign student that he shall apply one or more of these necessary rules in a flash when he is reading from a phonetic text. Another weighty

THE DIPHTHONGS ai AND aʊ

90. The symbol **a** is used with considerable scope: it may represent a central-front vowel (see Diagram and § 83), as in Northern E. *bad*,[1] or the first element in the diphthongs aɪ and aʊ. However, all the shades of vowel represented by **a** have this in common: they differ from the mixed vowels in that only one part of the tongue—the part close to the dividing line between front and back—is instrumental in forming them, whereas in the mixed vowels both front and back help to do so.

In the diphthong aɪ, as in *light*, the **a** is somewhat advanced from the centre and raised,[2] and the tongue rises to high-mid-

argument against the employment of a broad transcription is that a pupil may have a very keen ear for the varieties of a sound, and finds the broad transcription an inadequate medium in which to record them.

The main argument in favour of using a broad transcription is set forth in § 188.

Finally with regard to the various forms of the vocal murmurs to be heard in good speech, some speakers make hardly any difference in *quality* between the ə in *about, jealous, seldom* and the long ɜ in *bird*; for the latter sound they have a raised ɜ when it is fully long, i.e. ɜːˈ, but a distinctly lowered ɜ when it is unstressed and at the end of a breath-group (i.e. ɜ⊤), as in *over, sofa*; for this latter sound the narrow symbol ɐ could be employed, the sound approximating to a lowered and advanced ʌ (see scheme, p. 47). Such speakers make less difference between the two vowel-sounds in *murmured* than between the two vowel-sounds in *murmur*, the former being mɜːˈməd, the latter mɜːˈmɐ. In other words, their *bird*-vowel when shortened is almost identical with the ə vowel in *method*. (See the revised edition of Daniel Jones's *The Pronunciation of English*, now in the press.)

[1] This is the commonest form of **a** in Northern E., but there is also a form of it that approximates to ɑ, i.e. an advanced ɑ, or ɑ⊢.

[2] Here Dutchmen generally have too retracted and low a vowel, with lowering of the soft palate and consequent nasalization, so that they pronounce *light* as lãɪt. The same fault can be heard in some English dialects, notably cockney and "the Birmingham twang". This nasalizing of aɪ is difficult to cure; one device is to get the pupil to make the first

front, while in aʊ, as in *house*, the a is slightly retracted from the centre and raised, and the tongue rises to high-mid-back, the a in aʊ lying somewhere along the line between a and ʌ (cf. the Diagram). Considerable care must be taken by foreign speakers not to make either a too retracted or too deep.

90.1. If we compare English *house* with German *Haus* (hɑʊs), we shall find that the first element in the German diphthong is more retracted and slightly lower; a lessening of the mouth-opening helps to counteract this. The German diphthong is also longer than the English one.

Most foreign students have much difficulty in acquiring a satisfactory aʊ diphthong when learning English in England, and the cause is not far to seek. Instead of using aʊ, many English speakers use æʊ. This is generally termed the cockney form of aʊ; but it has such a wide distribution that careful speakers of St. E. must continually be on their guard, lest they get into the way of using it themselves.

90.2. While on the one hand there is an increasing tendency among the educated classes to advance the a in aʊ to the æ position, thus helping to establish this as the standard form, there is fortunately, on the other hand, an improvement on the part of the lower classes in the pronunciation of this diphthong. They are abandoning such cockney forms as əbaˑt or əbæˑt for *about*, flaˑz or even flæˑz for *flowers*. Soon, we may venture to hope, such a distortion as aˑz ɪz ə naɪs aˑs, æˑz ɪz for *ours is a nice house, ours is* may belong to past history.

element like ɛ, i.e. using a "mincing" diphthong as is done sometimes in the ultra refined pronunciation affected by ladies; once the nasalizing has been eradicated, the correct sound can be produced.

For another typical mistake made by Dutchmen, see § 203.

OTHER DIPHTHONGS

91. We have already considered the diphthongs heard in *made*, *road*, *hide* and *how*. We have also noted that ɛ̀ only occurs in St. E. as an element in the diphthong ɛɜ, as in *fair* (fɛɜ), *fairy* (fɛɜrì); in Scotch E. a long tense vowel is used here, and the r sounded even finally: fɛ́:r.

92. ɔɪ, as in *boy*. The first element is not ɒ, but ɔ raised to low-mid. An older form of this diphthong, oɪ, is still kept in some dialects, so that to a speaker of St. E. the dialectal *boy* sounds much like *bowie*, *joy* like *Joey*. In St. E. ɔɪ has developed in the colloquial pronunciation of *drawing-room*,[1] i.e. drɔɪŋrʊm for drɔˑɪŋruˑm, which latter persists for a room in which drawing is taught. In careless or rapid speech lɔɪɜ may be heard for lɔ:jɜ (*lawyer*).

93. English vowels tend to become diphthongal when lengthened, u: and i: becoming almost uːw and iːj. Sweet, in fact, used the transcriptions uw and ij for them; but this encourages a fault Scandinavians are already prone to make. Forms like duwɪŋ, sijɪŋ are to be deprecated, as they exaggerate the faint glide between vowel and suffix. The St. E. long u: begins lax, gets tenser, and ends in a faint w; long i: also begins lax, gets tenser, and ends in a faint -j sound. u: therefore stands for the equation ʊuᵂ, i: for ɪiʲ, so that i: and u: must be accepted as conventional symbols for a series of tongue-movements.

94. More clearly diphthongal are eⁱ and oᵘ when occurring finally in a stressed syllable or before a voiced consonant. The diphthongal forms are hard to imitate by speakers who have

[1] In the word *room* the modern tendency is to shorten the vowel to a half-long uˑ in the sense "apartment", and keep full length for the word in the sense "space". A short lax ʊ may often be heard in compounds, *bedroom*, *drawing-room*, etc. In *broom*, *groom* long u: is still in favour, in *bridegroom* shortening is fairly common.

long pure vowels in such cases, i.e. Scotsmen and Frenchmen. They are inclined to substitute for them tense eː and oː, sounds that a speaker of St. E. has great difficulty in acquiring.

95. The first element of the diphthong in *here* is either a retracted and laxly articulated i, or the high-drop ɪ. In distinct utterance the former seems to prevail, so either transcription will serve. But in the word *year* many speakers substitute jɜː for the older form jiɜ.

96. The first element of the diphthong in *poor* is usually ʊ except after j, when its place is taken by a retracted lax u, as in *cure, endure*, though many speakers use ʊ in this position as well. But in the word *your* the diphthong has been replaced by a long ɔ in the pronunciation of many speakers of St. E., who keep juɜ to represent the contraction *you're*. By analogy with *your*, possibly, such pronunciations as pɔː for *poor* and ʃɔː for *sure* can be heard, and even dʒɔːrɪ for *jury*; but these forms sound affected, clerical, or theatrical. In some dialects the older forms of *your*, joɜ and joɜ, still persist.

97. In provincial speech, ɑː and ɔː are diphthongized, the vowels finishing in a voiced off-glide, ɑːᵊ and ɔːᵊ, not in a light puff of breath as in St. E. In American E. this off-glide is a distinct murmur with the point of the tongue curled up to form a coronal vowel (see § 127) and the preceding vowel is shortened, *far more* becoming fɑɹ moɹ. The pure long vowels are characteristic of Standard speech, in which they have now established themselves with the majority of speakers.

98. aɪ and aʊ followed by a murmur, as in *fire, hour*, are sometimes referred to as triphthongs; but in St. E. true triphthongs[1] are very rare. A true triphthong is a succession of

---

[1] We hear one in *Irish* (aɪᵊrɪʃ), but not in *Ire-land* (aɪɜlənd). In the latter we have aɪ followed by ɜ. aɪrɪʃ is provincial.

three vowel-sounds which together combine to produce one sound, not a diphthong followed by a murmur. In poetry, however, such words as *fire* and *hour* count as monosyllabic—which they once were, when the r was still sounded.

OBSCURED VOWELS

99. In addition to the clearly recognizable vocal murmurs there are vowel-sounds intermediate between vocal murmurs and the vowels from which they have sprung. This is especially noticeable in careful or precise speech. Such obscured vowels, lying midway between full vowels and vocal murmurs, are not common in rapid conversation, but very common in speech that is clear without being pedantic. They can be rendered in phonetic script by means of the symbol for the unreduced vowel with the modifier ¨ over it. Thus, intermediate between səpoᵘz and sʌˈpoᵘz is the compromise säˈpoᵘz. Similarly in the unstressed vowels in *vineyard* (**vɪnjäˑd**), *disöbey*, *tö-night*, *sälinity*. Note how often an obscured æ tends to assert itself before double consonants in an unstressed initial position: *äccount, äccept, ädmit, ässumption, änticipate.*

100. These intermediate vowels are not easy to imitate, but the signs suggesting them might with advantage be used more extensively in texts for junior pupils who can only slowly decipher a transcription. The slower a text is read, the fewer will be the vocal murmurs that have lost all resemblance to the vowels from which they have originated. But in quick reading, the neutral murmurs become almost innumerable. Now, most phonetic texts are transcribed for fairly rapid speech. When such texts are read slowly, with their innumerable vocal murmurs, the effect is painful to an English ear. A judicious use of intermediate vowels helps to counteract this.

As an example of how obscured forms of vowels may be employed in the Declamatory Style of reading aloud, I give a transcription[1] of the first four stanzas of Swinburne's *Adieux à Marie Stuart.*

kwiːnˑ—fŏ huz haʊs maɪ fɑːðəz fɔˑt
  wɪð hoᵘps ðæt roᵘz‿ænd fɛlˑ—
rɛd staˑ‿ŏv bɔɪhʊdz faɪərì θɔˑtʰ—
    fɛsˡwɛlː | — |
ðeⁱ geⁱv ðɛs laɪvˑz — ænd >aɪ | maɪ kwiːnˑ |
  hæv gɪvn‿ju ŏv maɪ laɪfˑ —
sɪŋ jɔˑ breⁱv staː | bɜːn haɪ bìtwiːn
  mɛnˑz‿straɪfˑ | — |
ðə straɪf ðæt laɪtn̩d raʊnd ðɛs spiəz |
  lɒŋ sɪns fɛl stɪlˑ — soᵘ lɒŋˑ |
hɑˑdlì meⁱ hoᵘp tʊ laˑst ɪn jiəz
  maɪ sɒŋˑ | — |
bʌt stɪl θru straɪf ŏv taɪm‿ænd θɔˑt |
  jɔ laɪt ɒn miˑ tuː fɛlˑ —
kwiːnː | — | ɪn huz neⁱm wi sæŋ ɔˑ fɔˑtʰ —
    fɛsˡwɛlː | — |

CARDINAL VOWELS

101. If we were concerned in this place with dialect forms, we should have to add very considerably to our collection of symbols and signs, especially in the way of modifiers. What possibilities exist here may be gauged from Sweet's books on phonetics, in which he mapped out the vowels with geometrical exactitude. Assuming nine mouth-squares, he divided each square into nine subdivisions, so that he postulated eighty-one vowel-sounds.

[1] It will be noticed that, apart from where extra-lax ì appears, an obscured vowel is marked in nine cases in the sixteen short lines, and that the featureless vocal murmur ə appears but twice, once as a glide (faɪərì). Of the marks indicating pauses, the dash shows intermediate length between the short pause | and the long one | — |. The sign > indicates a "clear" beginning. The length-marks after consonants show how length is used to produce dramatic effect; so also the aspiration after the t in two places.

To substantiate his theory, Sweet established what he called
"cardinal" vowels. In his *Handbook of Phonetics* (1877) he
wrote: "From the infinite degrees of height three are selected,
'high', 'mid', and 'low'. These distinctions apply equally to
back, mixed and front vowels, so we have altogether nine
cardinal vowel-positions". But as each of these cardinal vowels
could be represented in what he called a "narrow" and a
"wide" variety, the cardinal vowels became eighteen, and, if
rounded vowels are kept separate from unrounded ones, the
number becomes thirty-six. Omitting this last distinction,
Sweet's standard vowels appear as in this Table:

	Front	Mixed	Back	
Narrow Wide	G. s*ie* b*i*t	Sw. h*u*s val*ue*	G. g*u*t p*u*t	}high
Narrow Wide	G. s*ee* m*e*n s*ay*	G. g*a*be bett*er*	c*o*me f*a*ther	}mid
Narrow Wide	c*a*re m*a*n	b*i*rd a in h*ow*	s*aw* n*o*t	}low

The scheme is very interesting, and was a valuable contribution to the study of phonetics when it appeared. But, as in
the case with the vowel triangle, it reveals the danger of a hard
and fast scheme. Thus, the rigid distinction between "narrow"
and "wide"—which we may call tense and lax—only holds
good of the high vowels as a whole; about the others there is no
consensus of opinion, and Sweet himself revised his analysis of
them on more than one occasion. Sweet's mixed u in *value* was
already becoming old-fashioned when his scheme appeared, and
only lingers on dialectically. His vowel-sound in *bird*, though
possibly a shade lower than the present-day vowel in St. E.,
was not absolutely low, since the tongue must rise in the centre

to produce a mixed vowel at all, and his a in aʊ, as in *now*, can hardly have been a mixed vowel unless it differed very considerably from the present mode of production for this element of the diphthong in St. E. So also his placing of the ɛ in *care* among the low-front vowels was apparently in order to fill the gap in that pigeon-hole, just as the ɑː in *father* had to go into the mid-back compartment because the low-back one was already filled. It is always possible, however, that Sweet's ɑː was actually a vowel produced with a higher rise of the tongue than the present form of ɑː, which seems to be a comparatively recent development.

Nevertheless, despite its inherent defects, Sweet's vowel-scheme may be said to have worked very well in practice, and his cardinal vowels served as a useful scale for making comparisons with other vowel-sounds.

An attempt has been made in recent years to establish cardinal vowels that do not belong to any group of languages, but are chosen arbitrarily and spoken with certain rigid tongue positions, giving them a definite acoustic quality. Professor Daniel Jones has created one such set of static vowel-sounds, and gramophone records have been made of it. These are its geographical habitat. Those who wish to make use of this set of sounds must either have gramophone and record handy, to make sure of some particular sound, or they must have immediate access to one of the few trained teachers who have mastered these phones. But what value can these sounds, formed with rigid tongue positions, have for purposes of comparison? They are not even based on the part of the tongue instrumental in forming a normal vowel-sound, but on the general position of the tongue, and they ignore the inevitable movement made by the tongue in helping to articulate a spoken vowel-sound.[1] Any set of "cardinal" vowels based on typical tongue positions must therefore differ essentially from a set of vowels formed in the usual way. It follows that conclusions drawn with the help of such "cardinal" vowels need not necessarily be regarded as proven.

VI

CLASSIFICATION OF CONSONANTS

102. Whereas in the production of vowel-sounds the air passes through the mouth without friction of the breath, and is normally accompanied by vibration of the vocal cords, consonants are produced by checking or obstructing the breath through the medium of the lips, teeth, tongue, palate, nose, throat, or some combination of these organs, with or without vibration of the vocal cords.

103. Of the lip, or labial, sounds, b, p, m and w are bi-labial, i.e. produced by means of the two lips; f and v are labio-dental, or produced with lower lip against upper teeth. θ and ð are articulated on the teeth, and classed as predental. Postdental or alveolar are the consonants articulated on the gums or teeth-ridge; those articulated between the front of the tongue and the hard palate, ç and j, are called palatal; those produced between the back of the tongue and the soft palate, or velum, are called velar. Glottal, or produced in the glottis, are ? and h.

104. Consonants may also be classified according to the manner in which they are produced. Thus, by stopping the air-

---

[1] The infinitely varied movements of the various speech-organs may some day be made quite clear by experimental phonetics; at present we know all too little about them. The lengthening of a vowel-sound merely prolongs one phase in its production.

passage, as in the case of p and t, we get stops, generally called plosive consonants, though they may also occur as purely occlusive sounds, such as the p in *midshipman* or the t in *Etna*. Sounds produced by the forced escape and friction of the breath through a narrowed aperture are known as fricatives or continuants. For the semi-vowels j and w, cf. § 72, note 2.

The l sounds are produced by letting air pass at the side or sides of the tongue. When breath is forced through the nose we get the nasal consonants m, n and ŋ. Sounds trilled or rolled by means of the tip of the tongue, as r, or by the uvula, as ʀ, are called trilled.

105. Combining these two bases of classification we get this Table:

	Plosive	Fricative	Semi-vowels	Lateral	Nasal	Trilled
Bi-labial	p, b	ʍ	w		m	
Labio-dental		f, v				
Predental		θ, ð				
Post-dental	t, d tʃ, dʒ	s, z, ʃ, ʒ ɹ		l	n	r
Palatal		ç	j			
Velar	k, g	x		ɫ	ŋ	ʀ
Glottal	ʔ	h				

For the value of the consonant-symbols, see § 16. ç is the *ch* in German *ich*, x the *ch* in German or Scotch *loch*, ʔ the glottal plosive prefixed in German to words beginning with a vowel; *r* is the trilled *r*, ʀ the velar sound as heard in Paris and elsewhere on the continent, ɹ the fricative *r* used in St. E. when *r* is not intervocal. ʍ is the voiceless form of *w* common in Ireland and some of the English dialects. ɫ is the "thick *l*"; see § 117.

106. Note in the Table above that the postdental sounds ʧ and ʤ are classed as plosives, because there is a single action of the tongue in articulating them. For the same reason the symbols should appear ligatured, if possible. The unligatured symbols can then be reserved for those compounds in which a postdental stop, or occlusive consonant, is followed by a postdental fricative, as in *Wiltshire* (wɪltʃɜ), *lightship* (laɪtʃɪp), *potsherd* (pɒtʃɜ·d), etc.

The initial and final consonant sounds in *church* are not quite identical: in the former the tongue assumes the ʧ position before articulation begins; in the latter there is a t stop after the vowel, followed by the plosive ʧ. Similarly with initial and final ʤ in *judge*, the initial consonant-sound being ʤ, the final one a d stop immediately released by ʤ; if this d before ʤ is not immediately released, the ʤ becomes voiceless.

We have a further proof of this contention that ʧ and ʤ cannot be regarded as having a fricative element when we find their effect on the length of a vowel-sound preceding them to be exactly the same as that of the plosive consonants, i.e. that ʧ ranks with p, t and k in reducing vowels to their shortest possible length, and that ʤ ranks with all single voiced consonants except liquids in lengthening "long" vowels to their utmost extent.

107. The classification of the nasal consonants only roughly indicates their formation. m is produced with closed lips, n and ŋ with lips not closed; but in the two latter cases the mouth-passage is closed by means of the tongue, which closes the passage for n by the blade of the tongue touching the teeth-ridge, and for ŋ by the back of the tongue pressing against the velum. In all three cases voiced breath is forced through the

nose, and the velum is lowered. If the phone were not voiced, nothing would result but breathing.

108. The distinction between voiced and voiceless sounds (see § 43) is of great importance in dealing with consonants. We have already seen that the length of a vowel can be influenced by the nature of the consonant-sound following in the same syllable (§ 81). Voicing is an essential part of any normal English vowel, but it is an essential part of certain consonants only, so that the beginner must learn to distinguish voiced consonants from voiceless ones. For voiceless some writers employ the term "breathed", but the expression is somewhat misleading: h is more purely a breath consonant than any other—it is "rough breathing"—and yet it is voiced very commonly when it occurs between two vowels.

109. There are various devices for proving to children that they are uttering a voiced consonant, such as laying the hand on the Adam's apple, or on the top of the head, or putting the hands to both ears. They can soon be taught to distinguish correctly between a voiced consonant and a voiceless one. And, as voiceless consonants are less sonorous than voiced ones, more force of breath is used in producing them.

In St. E. we can group voiced and voiceless consonants in these pairs:

$$\begin{cases} \text{p, t, ʧ, k, f, θ, s, ʃ, ç—voiceless,} \\ \text{b, d, ʤ, g, v, ð, z, ʒ, j—voiced.} \end{cases}$$

Voiced and unpaired in St. E. are l, ł, m, n, ŋ, r, ɹ and w. h is only voiced between two vowel-sounds.

110. Foreigners who have difficulty in making a clear distinction between s and z, ʃ and ʒ, must articulate the voiceless sounds sharply (see note to § 139), as well as practise using the voiced ones in the right place. The voiced varieties give most

trouble when they come intervocally, as in *position, preserve, imposing, resemble, vision, occasion, measure, hosier* (ho^{u}ʒɜ), *glazier* (gle^{i}ʒɜ). The difficulty is aggravated when English z is written *ss*, as in *dissolve, possess, dessert, hussar* (hʊˈzɑ:), *scissors* (sɪzɜz). A welcome reform would be to write these words *dizolve, pozess, dezert, huzar, scizzorz,* even if this might shock the susceptibilities of old-fashioned people.[1] But here we are primarily concerned with sounds, and not with the inconsistent way in which English is spelt—or spelled.[2]

111. Written *wh* is often pronounced as a voiceless sound in Northern E., especially in Ireland; the proper symbol for this is an inverted *w*, but as this is troublesome to write, a broad form **hw** is generally written instead, though **hw** really represents a third variety of *w*, viz. "rough breathing" prefixed to a voiced **w**. But neither of these two varieties of **w** is used by speakers of St. E., to whom the spellings *w* and *wh* connotate the same sound.[3] But in Belfast they would smile at anyone who pronounced *Whig* as *wig*, or *which* as *witch*. Speakers to whom the voiceless **w** is an unaccustomed sound, generally say **hw** when they try to imitate it, which they sometimes do when asked if there is any difference between *which* and *witch*, etc. To show the difference they will produce an artificial sound in order to prove that they know how certain words are spelled. Teachers often do this.

[1] The English name for *z* is zɛd in England, zi: in America. The older name for it, "izzard", from Middle English *ezed*, was more satisfactory in bringing out the voicing, as it stood intervocally.

The Swedish name for *z*, "säta" with voiceless s, suggests to the uninitiated Swede that *z* is merely another symbol for s.

[2] In St. E. the pronunciation spɛld means "cast a spell upon".

[3] Written *w* is always mute in *who, whose, whom* and *whole*. In *whole* there is no justification for the *w*, as in Middle English the word was written *hole*.

112. A voiceless consonant that plays a small part in St. E. is ç. It may be heard initially in a fairly normal modern pronunciation of the words *huge, Hugh, hue, human, humanity*, which seems to be displacing the hj in these words, a spelling pronunciation from older j.[1] The voiceless ç should be of particular interest to teachers who have difficulty in getting pupils to pronounce the *ch* in German *ich*: once the pupil grasps that the sound is employed in some English words, he soon manages to produce it himself. A ç may also develop from j by assimilation when following a voiceless consonant and coming before uː, as in *tumult, Tuesday, puny, accuse, fortitude, tube*, etc. In these words the u is advanced as compared with the u in *rude* (see also § 183).

113. The *l* and *r* sounds and the nasal consonants are conveniently referred to as liquids. They are normally voiced in St. E., but in certain positions they may become partially or even wholly voiceless, as in *clear, lamp, sneer, hint, length, try, pray*; the symbols to indicate this are l̥, m̥, n̥, r̥ and ŋ̊, but it is seldom necessary to mark this in transcriptions, since the majority of those whose mother tongue is a Germanic one mechanically unvoice a liquid after a voiceless consonant. Not so, however, speakers of Romanic languages; for them such transcriptions as kl̥iɜ may be useful.

114. Initially and finally, voiced consonants, with the exception of syllabic liquids, are only partially voiced in St. E.: in *deed* the d starts voiceless initially and ends voiceless finally. In this respect English stands midway between French and German: the French voice such sounds throughout, with the

[1] Bernard MacDonald in his *English Speech To-day* (1927) wrote: "Either ç or j may be said at the beginning of *humour*; ç is, perhaps, the more common nowadays, and is likely to become the established pronunciation in a few years' time".

exception to be noticed, while in German voiced consonants
other than liquids do not occur finally. Syllabic liquids in
English are heard in the words *chasm* (kæzm), *vision* (vɪʒn),
people (piːpl), in which the liquid that follows finally on another
consonant forms a syllable by itself, and acts as a vowel-sub-
stitute.[1] In such a position the final consonant-sound in French
and many other languages is merely whispered.

115. In most cases it is unnecessary to put a special mark
under the syllabic consonant in English, its commonest position
being final after another consonant-sound, as in *listen* (lɪsn),
saddle (sædl). But when a vowel follows in the same breath-
group, the syllabic consonant must be marked, as in *gluttony*
(glʌtn̩ɪ), *Sydenham* (sɪdn̩əm), *shovelling* (ʃʌvl̩ɪŋ), *certainly* (sɜ·tn̩lɪ),
occasionally (ö‖keⁱʒn̩lɪ). Cf. *chutney* (two syllables) with *gluttony*
(three syllables). When a syllabic nasal consonant follows a
plosive consonant, the release of the plosive is often made by
letting the stopped breath explode nasally. This is "nasal
plosion". In other words, the nasal serves as the outlet for the
plosion, and if the lips and tongue are kept in the same position
as they had for forming the plosive, the resultant nasal consonant is determined by this position. Thus, after a bi-labial
plosive the resultant nasal consonant would be m̩, as in *cup and
saucer* (kʌp m̩ sɔːsɜ), after a velar plosive it would be ŋ̍, as in
second (sɛkŋ̍d); but after a postdental plosive the lips and tongue
being already in the right position for articulating n̩ the plosive
can have no assimilating effect on the nasal sound. For the
avoidance of m̩ and ŋ̍ in such cases, see § 120.

116. All voiced consonants can be unvoiced, though some
of the voiceless forms are not used in St. E. unless they stand
in certain positions where they are affected by assimilation with

[1] This is not the same as a semi-vowel; see § 72, note 2.

a voiceless consonant, as pointed out in § 113. But in Welsh voiceless *l* and *r* are regular features of the language, are written *ll* and *rh* and pronounced ḷ and hr̥, as in *Llanelly* (ḷanˈɛḷi), *rhwd* (hr̥uːd). In Welsh the ḷ is generally a unilateral sound, i.e. only one side of the tongue is instrumental in producing it. The English ł after a plosive is usually a bilateral sound, and the resultant consonant, as in *battle* (bætl), serves as an outlet for the plosive part of the preceding consonant. This is known as lateral plosion (see § 121).

117. The *l* sounds in English are not easy to classify. One characteristic variety of English *l* is the one heard when lateral plosion takes place. This "thick *l*", as in *cobble*, *wriggle*, has a noticeable resemblance to the high-back vowel **u**, as in *cool*, the reason being that for ł the back of the tongue is drawn up as in forming **u**; at the same time the air-passage is partially closed by the blade of the tongue being held against the teeth-ridge, the front of the tongue is hollowed, and the air escapes at the sides of the tongue.

Another variety of *l* is heard when l stands between two forward vowels, as in *shilling*; the tongue-position here is naturally forward, and the result is a "clear *l*". Between "thick *l*" and "clear *l*" various intermediate forms can be heard: one such is used in St. E. when l is followed by a consonant-sound, as in *filled*, *belt*. Scotsmen often have ł here, likewise most Dutchmen and many Germans. This is a troublesome fault to deal with. The essential thing is to make the l that follows a vowel harmonize with that vowel; to use ł after a front vowel quite ruins the quality of the vowel-sound, a retracted l having such a marked influence on the preceding vowel. Native as well as foreign speakers must always remember that a promiscuous use of ł is much worse than not using it

at all, and that the "thick *l*" should only be employed when 1
occurs finally after a consonant-sound; to use it elsewhere
produces a very ugly effect, and it has very aptly been dubbed
the "throttled *l*".

118. The puff of breath that accompanies the release of the
plosives p, t, k when followed by a stressed vowel, as in *part*,
tug, *cat*, is too slight to be specially marked in the transcription;
the phonetic device for indicating it, should it be called for, is
to write p^h, t^h, k^h in such cases. But any excessive aspiration
of consonants, especially when they are final, is in English a
sign of unnatural or unrefined speech, as when a cockney says
dʌk^h (*duck*) with an explosive k, or is an affectation practised
by some clergymen and public speakers, as when they pronounce
a very emphatic and forcible *and* ænd^h. Many foreign speakers
do this unconsciously (see § 197).

Initially, strong articulation of consonants of the plosive class
is regular in Danish, frequent in German, but unnatural in
Standard French. In English, voiceless consonants are more
forcibly articulated than voiced ones, but the aspiration is not
strong. The proper degree of aspiration is thus an integral part
of good speech.

119. Compared with the t and d sounds in most other languages,
English t and d are retracted, i.e. the point of the tongue is
drawn back in articulating them. This can be indicated phonetically by writing them t⊣ and d⊣. The same peculiarity exists
in the speech of Finlanders, and is a regular feature of the
Swedish spoken in Finland.

Another parallel to a consonant-sound typical of St. E. exists
in the soft, untrilled r—the fricative sound—that is used by
many speakers of Spanish in South America, e.g. Chilians. But
the *r* sounds suggest so many problems that they must be
relegated to a chapter of their own.

A NOTE ON NASAL PLOSION

120. With regard to the employment of ən rather than n̩—and, of course, rather than m̩ after a bi-labial plosive, or ŋ̩ after a velar plosive (see § 115)—we may formulate the general principle that nasal plosion is avoided if awkward combinations of consonants would result, as in *London* (lʌndən), *husband* (hʌzbənd), *molten* (moᵘltən), *Gladstone* (glædstən), *question* (kwɛstʃən). Where no awkward consonant-group would result, but possibly an ugly or indistinct one, I find myself putting in the supporting ə more often than not after p and b—to avoid pm̩ and bm̩; after k and g—to avoid kŋ̩ and gŋ̩; and after ʧ, ʤ and l. Examples: *happen* (hæpən), *ribbon* (rɪbən), *bacon* (beⁱkən), *Wigan* (wɪgən), *pigeon* (pɪʤən), *fortune* (fɔːʧən), *woollen* (wʊlən). My nasal plosion therefore follows most commonly upon t and d, f and v, s and z, and ʃ and ʒ. Examples: *Brighton* (braɪtn̩), *garden* (gɑːdn̩), *soften* (sɔˑfn̩), *given* (gɪvn̩), *lesson* (lɛsn̩), *reason* (riːzn̩), *nation* (neⁱʃn̩), *vision* (vɪʒn̩). Inconsistencies must, however, be inevitable in everyone's speech; much depends on the style and rate of utterance, and on variations in emphasis; but for distinct utterance the above hints may do.

A NOTE ON LATERAL PLOSION

121. With syllabic l, which is more sonorous than n̩, the necessity for inserting a supporting vowel rarely arises. Most speakers of St. E. pronounce *little* as lɪtl̩; so after other consonants, as in *apple*, *bubble*, *tickle*, *giggle*, *satchel*, *cudgel*, etc. A clearly articulated lɪtəl sounds affected or foreign. It is only when consonant-groups would arise that might sound indistinct, that a supporting vowel is inserted, as in *equal* (iːkwəl), or where a cluck might be induced, as in *mortally* (mɔːtəlɪ),

fatally (feˑtəlì), rather than mɔːtl̩ì, feˑtl̩ì. In such cases the insertion of the supporting vowel is necessary to ensure clear articulation.

VII

THE *r* SOUNDS

122. The commonest form of *r* in St. E. is the fricative sound heard in *rich*, *bread*, etc. For this the narrow symbol is ɹ, but this inverted *r* is so troublesome to write that the Broad symbol r is generally substituted for it. But if one symbol be used for two sounds, the fricative and the trilled, we must bear in mind that in St. E. the latter only occurs between two vowel-sounds in the same breath-group, as in *arrive, merry, emerald, better and better*, and that even so the trill is very slight, consisting usually of but one tap of the tongue. Some speakers, indeed, never trill the *r* at all. The trill or roll is far more distinct in Northern E., while in Scotland a very strongly trilled *r* is a characteristic feature of the Lowland Scotch dialect. A Scotch sergeant, drilling a squad of raw recruits, is reported to have issued this command: "On the second syllable of the word 'turrn', you all 'turrn'". We might reproduce his "turrn" phonetically by writing it tʌrːn̩, so that he had some justification for regarding it as a word of two syllables in his pronunciation.

123. The uvular *r*, symbol ʀ, often heard in Parisian speech, is a sound produced by the vibration of the uvula against the back of the tongue. It may be heard in Northumberland, and is known in England as "the Northumbrian burr". It was at one time quite widely distributed in Northumberland and Durham, but is now only common round Berwick-on-Tweed.

Another variety of uvular *r* is produced in the same part of the mouth but without vibration of the uvula. It may be heard by speakers with no other markedly Northern E. characteristics, and in England it does not appear to have any definite geographical habitat (see § 133).

Many speakers who have only a uvular variety of *r* find the greatest difficulty in mastering the trilled and fricative *r* sounds. I have known foreign students to practise at them for a fortnight before they had quite overcome the difficulty. There are various formulæ for helping them to arrive at the desired result, one of the most effective being the tədɑːtədɑːtədɑːtədɑː spoken with ever increasing rapidity; but, as in the case of many other phonetic problems, it is always advisable to give pupils a description of the method of production. This may be formulated as follows: Fricative *r* is articulated with the tip of the tongue pointing towards and almost in contact with the back part of the teeth-ridge, the whole tongue being retracted and the front of it hollowed; through this tiny aperture breath, accompanied by voice, produces the typical St. E. fricative *r*. We could therefore define the sound as: Voiced postdental fricative consonant, tongue retracted and with hollowed front and elevated tongue-tip. The detailed description often helps foreigners to acquire the sound when other devices fail and their powers of imitative production are not well developed.[1]

By comparison, uvular *r* is easy to acquire; even babies in the cradle produce it without any apparent effort, and rejoice in making this happy gurgle; but they are blissfully ignorant of the fact that the sound they utter so merrily in the cradle may have to be learnt afresh with considerable trouble at a later stage of existence, for the flexibility of the tongue and uvula decrease with the passage of time.

[1] See also § 134.

124. The letter *r* has become mute in St. E. when followed by another consonant, as in *arc, word.* Where it was once sounded finally after a vowel it has either become mute, as in *fir,* or remains as a murmur or off-glide, as in *hear, fire, care, poor.* The glide has been absorbed by the preceding vowel in the cases exemplified in *stir, star, pour,* where pure long vowels have resulted, stɜː, stɑː, pɔː, in St. E., though in dialects the glide still persists. Intervocal *r* has remained, as in *stirring* (stɜˑrɪŋ), *faraway* (fɑˑrəweⁱ), *pouring* (pɔːrɪŋ). Where a glide-vowel remains before intervocal *r*, it is a less sonorous phone than the murmur that stands in a final position after the diphthongs aɪ and aʊ: compare *fire* (faɪɜ) with *firing* (faɪərɪŋ), *flower* (flaʊɜ) with *flowery* (flaʊərì). The same phenomenon can be observed in the vocal murmur element of diphthongs: cf. *hear* (hiɜ) with *hearing* (hiərɪŋ), *care* (kɛɜ) with *caring* (kɛərɪŋ), *cure* (kjʊɜ) with *curious* (kjʊərjəs).

125. Though *r* has become mute in St. E. before another consonant, it has left its mark on the nature or length of the preceding vowel-sound in most cases, creating the diphthongs ɪɜ, ɛɜ and ʊɜ, the long vowel ɔː from earlier ɔɜ, the long ɑː from earlier aɜ from the Late Middle English ar in *far,* and levelling under one form the five different sounds written *ir, ear, er, or* and *ur* in *bird, earth, err, word* and *burn.* In all such cases St. E. has achieved a more radical change than any other type of educated English speech, and herein lies its most clearly distinguished feature.

126. Though the lost *r* has left its mark on a preceding vowel-sound, it has left none on the consonant that follows it. In *lord* the d is sounded in the same way as after any other long vowel, and in *worst* the s is the same as in *past.* Swedes from Svealand (Sweden proper) use supradental d and s in similar

cases, and therefore pronounce the English word *person* with a supradental s—symbol ṣ—making it sound to an English ear like ʃ, i.e. pɜːʃn, which is the normal transcription of the word *Persian*. In this connection the most dangerous vowel is ɜː, since it has invariably developed from some vowel plus *r*, and is always written so in the nomic spelling. This written *rs* tempts the Swede to reproduce his supradental ṣ. The same temptation arises with other vowels, of course, as in *cars*, *course*, *Boers*, etc.

The substitution of ṣ for s is obnoxious to an English ear because it flavours of the speech of someone under the influence of alcohol, who will turn "Of course he is" into vkɔːʃjɪz, "twenty-seven" into twɛlʃɛbm, "what's the matter" into wɒʃmædʒ, "Queen's Road" into kwiːʒro, etc.

Obnoxious for the same reason are the American pronunciations with slack and half-formed t, as in sædʒdɪ or særʒdɪ for sætɜdɪ.

127. In American E., and in some English dialects, the consonant r after a vowel has turned that vowel into a "coronal" or "cacuminal" vowel, which means that the vowel is produced with the tip of the tongue curled up towards the hard palate. Examples: *heard, there, farm,* hɜ̣ːd, ðɛʒ, fɑʒm. A distinction is made by such speakers between *saw* and *sore, law* and *lore, flaw* and *floor, father* and *farther*, etc.

128. The persistence of intervocal r in St. E. has led to the inserting of an r where there is no justification for it in the spelling. Examples: "The Indiar Office; the idear of it; put a commar after it; a dramar on Samson; put your umbrellar up; chinar ornaments; sodar and milk; a vanillar ice". This insertion of an unjustifiable r is so common among speakers of good English that it is almost sanctioned by usage. But foreigners who are not tempted to insert this intercalated r are strongly

advised to avoid it. Careful speakers of St. E. manage to avoid
it by making a tiny pause at the junction of the two vowel-
sounds.

129. The reason why this intercalated r so doggedly intrudes
is that Englishmen are accustomed to inserting some sort of
glide between vowel-sounds coming together in the same breath-
group. After i the natural glide is a very faint j, as in *he is*,
after u and o a faint **w**, as in *are you in?*, *hoeing*, while after ɜː
ɛɜ etc. the consonant **r** is always at hand to fill the gap (§ 124).

Instead of a glide in such positions, many foreign speakers
are prone to insert a glottal plosive, ʔ, as in hiˑʔɪz, but the
glottal plosive is exceedingly rare in normally articulated St. E.
(see § 170).

130. The combinations **tr** and **dr** are difficult English sounds
for most foreigners to imitate successfully, the point of the
tongue being already drawn up against the teeth-ridge for the
t or **d**, so that for the production of the **r** it is only drawn back
slightly and hollowed, with the result that there is some resemblance between **tr** and **tʃ**, and between **dr** and **dʒ**: to make a clear
distinction between *chicory* and *trickery* the *ch* must consequently
be sharply articulated.

131. Among Irish speakers the position of the tongue for the
t in **tr** is against the teeth, the resultant sound for **tr** in such a
word as *true* being much like **tθruː**, and it is often written *thr*
in books that try to indicate the pronunciation of an Irish
character, as when Thackeray writes *thrifling, athrocious*.

132. We have noted that the *r* at the end of a word, always
mute in St. E. before a pause, as in *better*, may stand intervocally
in a breath-group, as in *better and better*, in which case, especially
in familiar expressions, the *r* is sounded. Some speakers sound
it consistently in such a position, unless an unpleasant effect

might be produced, as in *nearer and nearer*; others avoid sounding it when it follows ɑː or ɔː as in *a jar of jam, the war in the East, par of exchange, a store of anecdotes*. After ɛə, as in *a pair of shoes*, the general tendency is to insert **r**. But wherever the insertion of **r** in two consecutive syllables might produce cacophony, one of them is better omitted.

133. Distinct from this, though attributable to the same cause, is the omission of one of the two **r** sounds in the same word, as in the careless pronunciation of *February* as fɛbjʋərì, *temporarily* as tɛmpərəlì, *library* as laɪbərì, *secretary* as sɛkɪtərì. Careful speakers always articulate both **r** sounds in such words. Here faulty pronunciation is induced by the difficulty of articulating two **r** sounds so close together. But what excuse can be found for the quite incomprehensible distortion of the **r** sounds to be heard in the speech of many public school boys in England at the present time, who, with infinite difficulty, learn to produce a sound that is considered to be "classy"? It is not an unrounded **w**, but rather an unvoiced ʀ.[1] It is to be hoped that this affectation will soon die a natural death. The monstrosity should be made a punishable offence.

134. The difficulty of initial **r**, which is always a fricative in St. E. speech, may be overcome by lip-rounding, as though **r** were preceded by a **w** in glideless combination, **wr**: (*w*)*read*, *t*(*w*)*ry*,

---

[1] As in Danish. Symbol ʀ. The foregoing paragraphs do not lay claim to having exhausted all the possibilities that exist in the varieties of *r*-sounds that can be heard in the speech of foreign students. But one more substitute may be referred to before taking leave of this troublesome consonant. The curious Japanese **r**, with its similarity to an **l**, though *l* does not exist in Japanese, is due to the contact of the tongue with the teeth-ridge in the act of articulation. This imitation of both *l* and *r* is a kind of compromise between the two sounds. But that this is not an exclusively Oriental peculiarity can be heard in the dialect of Östergöt-land, Sweden, which has a similar hybrid.

b(w)read.[1] The peculiarity of the English sound is probably due to the long persistence of consonantal **w** in Germanic words beginning with *wr-*. The alliteration *ríche:reccheo* in the *Hildebrandslied* shows that **w** before *r* was lost in High German before A.D. 800, but 600 years later it still appears to retain its full consonantal value in English, for in *Piers Plowman*, c. 1377, we find *wrath* alliterating with *wedding*, *work*; *wrought* with *wedding*, *woe*, *wit* and *worse*; *write* with *windows*, *well*, etc. Presumably the vestigial lip-rounding was subsequently generalized by analogy. Is there any other language in which children commonly substitute **w** for initial **r**?[2]

VIII

LENGTH OF VOWELS AND CONSONANTS, AND THEIR INTERRELATION: WEAK FORMS OF WORDS

135. We have seen (§ 81) that in short,[3] stressed words the vowel is longer before a voiced than before a voiceless consonant, unless it be a short vowel other than æ before a liquid, or a long vowel before l or a liquid supported by a voiceless consonant.

For short vowels the following pairs further illustrate § 81.2:

| *hiss* | *pith* | *rook* | *beck* | *buff* | *mop* | *Scotch* | *ass* | *cap* | *batch* |
| *his* | *with* | *good* | *beg* | *above* | *mob* | *dodge* | *as* | *cab* | *badge* |

These vowels, except æ, remain short before liquids: *pill*,

---

[1] Neutral lip-position appears to favour velar *r* or a harsh inverted *r*.

[2] For the above paragraph on lip-rounding with initial English r I am indebted to Dr Perrett.

[3] For the length of the stressed vowel in words of two or more syllables, see § 81.4.

pull, hen, stem, don, song, sung, pun; but the liquids themselves become long in such cases: pɪlː, etc. For the length of short vowels before consonant combinations, see § 138; for the length of the consonants, see §§ 139–141.

136. The long vowels and diphthongs are fully long in short, stressed words before the voiced consonants b, d, ʤ, v, ð, z and ʒ, or combinations of these consonants; nearly fully long when final or before a nasal not supported by a voiceless consonant; half-long before f, θ, s, ʃ, or combinations of these consonants, and before 1 not supported by a voiceless consonant; and nearly half-long before t, p, k, ʧ, or combinations of these consonants, or before a liquid supported by a voiceless consonant. Here follow examples of long vowels and diphthongs before various consonants, or when final, arranged in the four columns of diminishing length:

iː	bead(s)	bee, beam	iˑ	beef	beak
	league(d)	lee, lean		leash	leech
ɜː	curb(ed)	cur, turned	ɜˑ	curse	curt
	purrs	purr, spurn		curl(ed)	burnt
				purse	perch
uː	rouge	rue, rune(s)	uˑ	Ruth	root
	lose	loo, loom		loose(d)	loop
ɑː	bard(s)	bar, balm	ɑˑ	bath	bark
	barb	darn(s)		marl(ed)	dance
ɔː	forge	fore, form(ed)	ɔˑ	forth	fault
eⁱ	rave(d)	ray, rain		race	rake
	bathe(d)	range		rail(s)	quaint
oᵘ	road(s)	roe, roam		wroth	roach
	doze(d)	doe, dome(s)		dole(s)	dolt
aɪ	eyes	eye, lime(s)		ice	like
		nigh, nine		nice	ninth
aʊ	loud	plough, down		louse	lout
ɔɪ	joys	joy, join(ed)		rejoice(d)	joint

137. When a vowel gains length before a voiced consonant, the consonant itself loses in length. Contrariwise, when a vowel loses length before a consonant, the consonant itself gains in

length. Thus, in the upper row of the short vowels in § 135, the end consonants are longer than in the lower row. In *buff* the f is therefore longer than the **v** in *above*. In the two left-hand columns of the long vowels (§ 136) the end consonants in those words are quite short and almost whispered in the first column, shortened and only partially voiced in the second; in the third and fourth columns the consonants take up the length lost by the vowels, and in the fourth column they are articulated with considerable energy, though their length is obscured because it is largely taken up by the stoppage made by the plosives. With the fricatives in the third column, the vowel is not cut off so abruptly, and retains somewhat more length, though not so much as foreign students are apt to give it (cf. what is said at the end of § 81.2).

138. Short vowels except **æ** remain short before two consonant-sounds, whatever they may be. But, by the law of compensation, some length falls to one or both of these consonants. How is that length apportioned? Three categories arise: (1) when one of the consonants is a liquid; (2) when the supported consonant is voiced but not a liquid; (3) when the supported consonant is voiceless, and the supporting consonant is not a liquid.

139. (1) A liquid supported by a voiced consonant keeps its full length and the supporting consonant becomes unvoiced (whispered): *build* (bɪlːd̦), *pens* (pɛnːẓ), *sponge* (spʌnːd̦ʒ̣ or spʌnːʒ̣), *fringed* (frɪnːʒ̣d̦). When the supporting consonant is voiceless, the length is shared and the supporting consonant sharply articulated: *built, pence.*[1] When a liquid supports any

---

[1] The voiceless Scandinavian s differs from English s in being softer (not so sharply hissed), so that in *pence* such an s sounds too weak. This softer s differs so little from unvoiced ẓ in English *pens* that it is absolutely essential to observe the length of nː in *pens*.

other consonant, the two share the length: *runnel* (rʌnl), *model* (mɒdl), *chasm* (kæzm), *vision* (vɪʒn), *little* (lɪtl), *button* (bʌtn).

140. (2) The supported consonant other than a liquid is as a rule only followed by another voiced consonant,[1] and is lengthened, though not so much as a liquid would be, and the supporter becomes unvoiced (whispered): *buzzed* (bʌzˑd̥), *ribbed* (rɪbˑd̥), *dregs* (dregˑz̥), *ridged* (rɪdʒˑd̥).

141. (3) Voiceless consonant supported by another voiceless one. The supporting consonant, unless it be a liquid, can only be voiceless.

The supported consonant is slightly lengthened when it is a plosive, as in *cuts* (kʌtˑs), *books* (bʊkˑs), more distinctly lengthened when it is a fricative, as in *rushed* (rʌʃˑt), *lisp* (lɪsˑp), *cleft* (klɛfˑt).

When the supporting consonant-element is made up of plosive plus fricative, the effect on the supported consonant is the same as if the last consonant were absent: *depths* (dɛpˑθs) has very slightly lengthened p, while in *lisps* the s is as long as in *lisp*.[2]

142. In unstressed syllables long vowels and diphthongs lose much of their length, and tend to lose their diphthongal nature, eⁱ and oᵘ becoming e and o, which latter becomes obscured ö or is replaced in careless speech by a murmur, *innocent* (ɪnösənt) becoming ɪnəsənt, *abolition* (æböˈlɪʃn) becoming æbəˈlɪʃn (cf.

[1] Quite exceptionally by a voiceless consonant, e.g. in *breadth* and *width*: see § 184.
[2] The examples in §§ 136–141 can be used for practice quite apart from the categories in which they are placed. They may prove useful to the foreign student who has never observed the interrelation between vowels and consonants in the matter of length; very often, indeed, his pronunciation of English, excellent in many respects, leaves much to be desired in this particular; he may find a little extra attention to consonant length will be of greater service to him than the exact observance of such rules as exist for the length of English vowels.

§ 99); in careful speech the reduced e from e^i often passes into ɪ: in *advocate, candidate*, all three pronunciations may be heard, -e^{i}t, -et and -ɪt; ɪ is more usual than e in *holiday, yesterday, Sunday*, etc., and *always* is now usually ɔ·lwɪz. In proper names, *-gate* has become -gɪt, as in *Ramsgate, Harrogate*. In all such cases the substitution of ɪ for ɪ or e is a cockneyism (see § 73).

143. Still more important, because unexpected, is the retention of length and diphthongal quality in unstressed syllables; foreign students are prone to shorten the vowels in such words, and have difficulty in breaking themselves of the habit. Some examples are: *rhubarb* (ru·bɑ·b), *blackguard* (blægɑ·d), *female* (fɪ·me^{i}l), *series* (sɪəri·z), *conclave* (kɒnkle^{i}v), *cohort* (ko^{u}hɔ·t), *congeries* (kɒn'dʒɛrɪi·z) and the substantives *console*, (kɒnso^{u}l), *commune* (kɒmju·n).

In unstressed syllables ɪ is often substituted for the diphthong aɪ, though there seems to be no underlying principle to direct the change, other than linguistic usage. Thus, in *direct, finance, financier, financial* one hears ɪ more often than aɪ in the first syllable, whereas in *titanic* and *organization* the ɪ of the unstressed syllable seems to be dying out, and in *gigantic* only aɪ is now heard. *Finale* is fɪ'nɑ·lɪ. Considerable diversity can be heard in the pronunciation of the unstressed prefix *di-*; thus, *diversity* is daɪ'vɜ·sɪtɪ or dɪ'vɜ·sɪtɪ; similarly with *didactic, digest* (verb), *digression, dilemma, dimension, directly, director* and others; ɪ is perhaps preferable, save in *digression*.

Cases of extreme shortening in unstressed syllables are common in compound words that are no longer felt to be compounds, typical cases being *waistcoat* (wɛskət), *forehead* (fɒrɪd), *purchase* (pɜ·tʃɪs), *cupboard* (kʌbəd), *breakfast* (brɛkfəst), *saucepan* (sɔ·spən), *welcome* (wɛlkəm), *half-penny* (he^{i}pənɪ), *twopence* (tʌpəns), *three-pence* (θrɛpəns or θrɪpəns).

Nautical terms have undergone considerable shortening in the speech of sailors, and the forms used by them have been adopted in very many cases by the general public: such are *forecastle* (fo^uksl), *boatswain* (bo^usn), *gunwale* (gʌnl), *mainsail* (meⁱnsl), *studding-sail* (stʌnsl), *rowlock* (rʌlək), *taffrail* (tæfrəl), *leeward* (lju·əd), *sou'west, nor'wester*.

144. The weakened form sometimes helps to make a word unambiguous. The pronunciation ɔːlweⁱz for *always* might be taken to mean *all ways*, but ɔ·lwɪz is unambiguous; so, too, əgɛn is unmistakably *again*, which əgeⁱn is not, as it might mean *a gain*; sʌndɪ can be nothing but *Sunday*, whereas sʌn deⁱ could be confused with *some day*. A shortened vowel may also help to distinguish one part of speech from another: the verbs *estimate* (ɛstɪmeⁱt), *compliment* (kɒmplɪmɛnt or kɒmplɪˈmɛnt), *experiment* (ɪksˈpɛrɪmɛnt) differ thus from the substantives ɛstɪmɪt, kɒmplɪmənt, ɪksˈpɛrɪmənt, the verb *appropriate* (əpro^uprieⁱt) from the adjective əpro^uprɪɪt, etc. Note the different stressings and pronunciations of the words spelled *absent, conduct, desert, produce, rebel, minute, conjure*.

145. A difficult problem for foreigners is the right use of weakened forms of common words in reading and speaking. Here much should depend on the way words are grouped together. *I see him* is aɪ ˈsɪ·ɪm in ordinary speech; a distinct hɪm would sound emphatic, but if the slightest pause be made between *see* and *him* the form ɪm becomes offensive. The beginner is apt to read each word as an independent unit, and not, as he should do, as a member of a breath-group. Breath-groups should therefore be clearly indicated in phonetic transcriptions.

146. The words most frequently reduced to weak forms are the articles, personal pronouns, auxiliary verbs, especially in

conjunction with *not*, and the words *and, as, at, but, for, from, of, than* and *to*.

147. The definite article, the emphatic and isolated form of which is ði:, generally becomes ði before a vowel and ðə before a consonant; occasionally we can hear ðɪ before a vowel, as in *the army* (ðɪ ɑ:mi), and occasionally ði before a consonant-sound, as in *The United States* (ði junaɪˈtɪd steⁱts). In poetry the elision of the vowel in *the* practically reduces the word to ðj, as in Wordsworth's "She dwelt among the untrodden ways".

148. The pronouns *he, she, we, me*, when shortened retain the tense vowel, hi, etc. Actors alone take the liberty of using lax vowels here: in "Is this a dagger that I see before me?" the last word is often pronounced mɪ by them. Another mannerism affected by many actors is the use of mɪ instead of maɪ, as in "This is my own, my native land". In *my lord, my boy*, and a few other expressions, mɪ is usual.

149. A grammatical distinction can be observed in the two forms of the demonstrative, relative or conjunctional *that*; ðæt is demonstrative, ðət relative or conjunctional: *It's that that I require, and I know that I shall get it.*

150. Various degrees of shortening may be observed in the auxiliary verbs, the extreme case being d for *should* or *would*, as in "*I'd like to see him, and he'd like to see me*".

The contractions *hasn't, isn't*, etc. are very common in un-emphatic speech, but are avoided in print unless conversation is being reported. In conversation the occasion may influence the form employed; thus, in speaking to a dignitary of the Church, one would naturally avoid the form ʃɑ:nt and use ʃl nɒt, whereas hævnt would only be replaced by həv nɒt or (ə)v nɒt in somewhat emphatic statement, or as an instinctive protest against the excessive use of shortened forms in *n't*, which may jar on the

ear. Note that the old contractions haːnt for *have not* and eˡnt
for *am not* have become vulgarisms. Such a full form as *had
you not* is very rarely employed, its place being taken by
hadn't you, which latter preserves the old word-order. *Won't*
goes back to Middle English *wol not*, while the phrase *willy-nilly*
preserves·the Old English verb-form *nillan*, from *ne willan*,
"will not", still to be read as *nil* in Shakespeare's *Hamlet* and
The Taming of the Shrew.

151. A curious error has gained ground among many foreign
teachers of English with regard to the employment of shortened
forms. Perhaps deducing from Sweet's phonetic texts, after
comparing the transcribed forms with the transliteration of
those texts, that English speakers invariably employ the
shortened forms in reading a text aloud, they teach their pupils
to turn a brace of contractable words into the contracted form
on every possible occasion, so that the present tense of *have*
becomes aɪv, juːv, hiːz, wiːv, ðeˡv, even when the words occur
in descriptive prose. Everything, in short, is turned into
colloquial English, and the effect is dreadful.

152. Foreigners seem to fight shy of inserting vocal murmurs
in two consecutive unstressed syllables in long words. Thus, for
comfortable (kʌmfətəbl) they will persist in saying kʌmfɔteˡbl
with secondary stress on the third syllable, but this can only
represent *come for table* with faulty stressing. A phonetic transcription soon breaks them of this habit, which arises from their
trying to pronounce words as they are spelt.[1]

So-called spelling-pronunciations are not at all uncommon

---

[1] In light verse an unexpected full vowel is occasionally employed to
produce a comic effect, as when *intent* is rimed with *Monu-ment*, or in this
couplet from Horace Smith's *Tale of Drury Lane*:
> In borrowed lustre seem to sham
> The rose or red sweet Wil-li-am.

even with English speakers, common examples being undesirable forms of *spelled, decade, used to, bade, burned, ate, shone,* which should be spɛlt, dɛkəd, juˑst tʊ, bæˑd, bɜˑnt, ɛt, ʃɒn.[1] In some place-names the spelling has actually altered the pronunciation in its received form, as in *Sevenoaks, Pontefract* for older sɛnöks,[2] pʌmfrĭt, and many more.

IX

STRESS

153. Even in single words it is possible to distinguish many degrees of stress. If we take the word *ability,* we can hear that the strongest stress falls on the second syllable, the weakest on the third, and the next weakest on the first, or, to show this in figures we could say it has 2 : 4 : 1 : 3 stressing. But for practical purposes such accuracy is not called for. The main thing a student wants to know in learning a new language is which syllable in a word carries the chief stress. One way of indicating this in a phonetic text is to put a stress-mark before the stressed syllable. Thus, *indisputably* is pronounced inˈdɪspjutəblĭ, *irrevocably,* ɪˈrɛvokəblĭ. From these two examples it can be seen that stress tends to be shifted back in English. In *balcony* it has been shifted from the second to the first syllable, in *melancholy* from the third to the first. The shiftings since Shakespeare's time have been very few, those since Chaucer's time innumerable.

154. The chief objection to placing the stress-mark in front of the stressed syllable is that the stress may actually begin

---

[1] In *learned* or *learnt,* the imperfect and past participle of *learn,* the form lɜːnd lingers on beside the more usual lɜˑnt.

[2] Hence the somewhat prosaic proper name *Snooks.*

midway in the articulation of a consonant-sound, as in *distend*; neither *dis-tend* nor *di-stend* marks the exact place where the stressing begins, viz. in, not before or after, the s. Or, again, the stressed syllable may begin in the word preceding the stressed vowel, as in *not at all*, which is generally pronounced nɒtəˈtɔːl.

Sweet invented a somewhat complicated system of marking stress, but, as far as I can discover, it has found no imitators; it is perplexing to the reader. Apparently the perfect system of stress-marking has still to be devised: all those in present use are open to some objection.

155. No stress-mark is required in words with stress on the first syllable only, nor in words stressed on the second only where the first is incapable of being stressed, i.e. when the vowel in the first contains a short vocal murmur, ĭ, or an obscured vowel, such as ö. Thus ĭntræp (*entrap*) requires no stress-mark, but ĭnˈsait (*incite*) does, to distinguish it from ĭnsait (*insight*). The substantive *pervert* (pɜːvət) is stressed differently from the verb pəvɜːt, but no mark is required to show this.

156. Where it is expedient to mark secondary stress, this can be done by putting a secondary mark from the line downwards: *inferiority*, *individuality* (ɪnˌfiərɪˈɒrɪtĭ, ˌɪndɪˌvɪdjuˈælɪtĭ). Foreigners often ignore secondary stresses, and rush on to the strongly stressed syllable. But attention must be paid to the stressing of polysyllabic words.[1]

157. In compounds or words treated as such, there are three main types of stressing: stress on first element only, *gold-fish*; secondary stress on first element, strong on second, *backgammon*, *pocket-handkerchief* (ˌpɒkɪtˈhæŋkətʃɪf); level stress, which means equal stress on both elements, as in *archbishop* (ˈɑːtʃˈbɪʃəp).

[1] Daniel Jones's *Pronouncing Dictionary* is an invaluable reference work for secondary stress.

158. Apart from the problem of stress in the isolated word, there is the problem of stressing words that are intimately connected with one another. Here we may distinguish three main varieties: level or even stress, descending stress, and ascending stress. All three may be heard in one and the same word: we hear level stress in *unknown*, descending stress in *an unknown fact*, ascending stress in *quite unknown*.

159. It is level stress that causes most trouble. As it is practically non-existent in German, German speakers tend to pronounce *steel pen* with descending stress instead of level stress; Scandinavians do the same. Examples of level stress are: *Gloster Road, Hanover Square, Hyde Park, Edward Johnson*; of descending stress: *Oxford Street, house-agent, china-ware, Johnson and Co.*; of ascending stress: *New York, the Chinese, good evening, whatsoever*. With *House* stress is usually level, as in *Apsley House*; note the exceptional *Mansion House* with descending stress. *Churchyard* generally has descending stress, but in *St Paul's Churchyard* the stressing is level.

160. Contrasting stress may disturb the normal stressing, as in "He said *Hyde* Park, not *Regent's* Park"; "The one was an *assistant* master, the other a *head*-master"; "A happy beginning, but an *unhappy* ending"; "It is culture we want, not *over*-culture".

161. Words with level stress when isolated tend to have descending stress when they occur attributively before a substantive, ascending stress as adverbs; cf. *the inside of a hand, an inside passenger*, with *come inside*, in which last case the word is an adverb and stressed (–ˈ). Cf. further *a Chinese lantern* (–ˈ–ˈ–) with *the Chinese* (––ˈ), *5 o'clock tea* (ˈ––ˈ) with *5 o'clock* (ˈ–ˈ), *1740* (ˈ––ˈ–) with *he's 17* (–ˈ–ˈ), *the overhead railway* (–ˈ––ˈ–) with *just overhead* (ˈ––ˈ), *every-day life* (ˈ––ˈ) with

every day (|–|), *afternoon lessons* (|––|–) with *this afternoon*
(–|–|).

162. The examples just given reveal a rhythmic influence and
a tendency to avoid consecutively stressed syllables. This ex-
plains why one says *Waterloo* (|–|) but *Waterloo Bridge* (|––|),
a Seville orange (–|–|–) but *Old Seville* (|–|). The avoidance of
the awkwardly stressed *Trafalgar Square* (|–||) accounts for
the stressing (–|–|), and hence for the present stressing in
Trafalgar (–|–) itself. The old stressing is preserved in Wilde's
Ave Imperatrix:

> And some in Russian waters lie,
> And others in the seas that are
> The portals to the East, or by
> The wind-swept heights of Trafalgar.

163. We can understand the old lady's joy in "that blessed
word Mesopotamia": it was the rhythmic lilt that pleased her
ear. But it is not old ladies alone who fall under the spell of
rhythmic allurement: even prose-writers of distinction may be
beguiled by it. Dickens was, in his sentimental moods, and
Wilde was a frequent offender in this respect. In *The Old
Curiosity Shop* Dickens repeatedly drops into rhythmic prose,
but he was cognizant of it himself and even wrote to his friend
Forster expressly asking him to correct those passages where it
became evident. The letter is dated Nov. 13th, 1846.

On the other hand, Wilde seems to have aimed purposely at
achieving a rhythmic lilt in some of his prose works. In his
Fairy Tales there are whole passages which are practically
blank verse. Here is an example from *The House of Pome-
granates*: "The robe of tissued gold, and the ruby-studded
crown, and the sceptre with its rows and rings of pearls".

The same tendency can be seen in the prose of many others.

Even the great Thackeray, that practised master of prose, could be guilty at times of the same trick. It is seen in this passage from *Esmond*, where possibly the initial temptation resulting from an alliterative jingle leads on to more alliteration, and finally to blank verse: "She made dishes for his dinner; spiced his wine for him; made the toast for his tankard at breakfast; hushed the house when he slept in his chair, and watched for a look when he woke".

164. Stress is an essential factor in the building up of English verse; in prose it should be carefully distributed, so as to avoid monotony on the one hand, and rhythmical sequences on the other. It follows that the foreign student, reading from an ordinary text, where stresses are not indicated, is less likely to go wrong in stressing a passage of English verse than a passage of English prose; this is a cogent argument in favour of a more liberal use than is at present in vogue of English poetry in the schoolrooms abroad.

165. In poetry, stresses occur with a certain regularity. In the hands of an unskilful artificer, this may result in a dead monotony; with a master of his craft the monotony is smoothed over by an adept use of vowel and consonant sounds. Thus, in the opening couplet of Scott's *Lay of the Last Minstrel*, the vowel-sounds are alternately from a higher to a lower vowel in the stressed words: "The w*a*y was long, the w*i*nd was cold, the m*i*nstrel was inf*i*rm and *o*ld". The same may be seen in the first couplet in this stanza from Byron's *The Destruction of Sennacherib*, while in the second couplet the reverse is the case:

> For the angel of death spread his wings on the blast
> And breathed in the face of the foe as he passed,
> And the eyes of the sleepers waxed deadly and chill
> And their hearts but once heaved, and for ever grew still.

Vowel sequences can best be studied in blank, i.e. unrimed, verse, as the poet is free from the trammels of rime. An interesting study is afforded by W. Collins's *Ode to Evening*.

The beauty of long vowels and diphthongs in stressed words may be seen in the lines from Keats's *Ode to a Nightingale*:

> Perhaps the self-same song that found a path
> Through the sad heart of Ruth, when, sick for home,
> She stood in tears amid the alien corn;
> The same that oft-times hath
> Charm'd magic casements, opening on the foam
> Of perilous seas, in faery lands forlorn.

It is still more striking in the famous couplet from Christopher Marlowe:

> Oh, thou art fairer than the evening air
> Clad in the beauty of a thousand stars!

166. Almost equally important is the part played in the efficacy of poetry by the consonant-sounds in stressed syllables. If we take these lines of Tennyson's, from *The Lady of Shalott*:

> But who hath seen her wave her hand?
> Or at the casement seen her stand?
> Or is she known in all the land,
> The lady of Shalott?

we must attribute much of the charm and beauty of the lines to the length of the n sounds in the stressed words *hand, stand* and *land*. We can also note how the mid-line consonants in *seen, casement, known* help to reinforce them, and furthermore the alliterative effect of the l sounds in *all, land, lady, Shalott*. It is, in fact, almost an excess of dexterity to crowd so many poetic effects into four short lines, and it makes them somewhat oversugared.

167. Alliteration, in poetry and prose alike, helps to reinforce

or accentuate stressed words. It plays a big part in proverbs and familiar sayings, similes and household expressions. Here are a few well-known examples: "Dead as a doornail; As dull as ditchwater; Good as gold; Hale and hearty; Spick and span; Proud as a peacock; Pain past is pleasure; Smooth words make smooth ways; Fortune favours fools; Every country has its custom; Hanky-panky; Higgledy-piggledy; Hocus-pocus; Humpty-dumpty; Namby-pamby; Shilly-shally; Fiddle-faddle; Tittle-tattle; Topsy-turvy".

168. Some years ago, certain English newspapers, and quite a number of the sensational newspapers in U.S.A., were fond of alliteration in their scare-lines, but the apparent alliteration was often no alliteration at all, as can be seen when the heading "City Clerk Chased" is transcribed, sıtì klɑːk ʧeⁱst. J. K. Jerome made fun of this journalistic trick in one of his sketches, where he coined an amusing example, "Baby bitten by a baboon in a back street at Bow". Alliteration, like every other literary device, must be kept within bounds: it is pleasing in Swinburne's early poetry, wearisome in his later.

169. Alliteration played a great part in Old English verse, three of the four accented syllables in each line being inseparably connected by alliteration, i.e. they began with the same consonant-sound, or with vowels, though not the same vowel. From the circumstance that words beginning with different vowels were regarded as being in alliteration, it has been conjectured that in Old English, as in modern German, words beginning with a vowel were sounded with a glottal plosive, since such a line as "endless and on, ever to last" would lose much of its poetic force when deprived of the ictus it derived from the insertion of the glottal consonant. The argument against this is that the alliterative effect is just as strong with emphatic

initial voice: "When > Adam and > Eve > ate of the > apple".[1]
Even if one might quarrel with the dictum "just as strong",
emphatic initial voice is certainly more poetically effective. In
any case, my glottal plosive conjecture[2] has not met with
general acceptance.

X

THE GLOTTAL PLOSIVE

170. The glottal plosive is so unusual in St. E. speech that a
speaker of St. E.—or, for the matter of that, of any form of
English—finds it as hard to insert in speaking German as
many Germans find it hard to lay aside in speaking English.
It is occasionally employed by public speakers to give emphasis
(tə gɪv ʔɛmfəsɪs), and has lately become a mannerism among
some broadcasting announcers, who strive to make their speech
more distinct by barking some of the words. To assert, therefore,
that it is impossible to acquire, or difficult to imitate, is an
absurdity. It is indispensable for the purpose of coughing,
which might be transcribed ʔɜhə ʔɜ or ʔʌhʌ ʔʌ, or for very old
people ʔʊːhʊ ʔʊ. If they were told they were employing a
glottal plosive they might feel as much astonished as was
Monsieur Jourdain when he was informed by his professor that
he had been talking prose all his life.

171. A very slight glottal plosive is sometimes employed by
English speakers to avoid ambiguity. In the combination *three
ears* a glide is apt to insert itself between the two i sounds, the
resultant form θriˑjiəz closely resembling θriˑ jiəz, i.e. *three years.*

---

[1] Communicated by Dr Perrett.
[2] Professor Jespersen writes: "Axel Koch and myself have written
against this conjecture in my *Lehrb. der Phonetik*, p. 78[2]".

The former is consequently pronounced θriˑ ʔiɜz by speakers who have not a "clear beginning" for the vowel in *ears*. But such a glottal plosive is very weak in comparison with the forcible explosion used by many Germans, especially those from Holstein and eastwards. They must practise saying *three old owls* without checking the breath once in the process of articulation.

172. A glottal stop, as it is often called, is frequent in some of the English dialects, not as a glottal plosive, but as an occlusive, i.e. not a breath-explosion, but as a breath-check. In Glasgow, *water* is often pronounced with a glottal occlusive instead of the t, i.e. waʔɜ, and *bottle* as bɒʔl; more rarely it absorbs a p or a k. Scotland is apparently the chief habitat of this distortion, though it is also very common in cockney speech, and in provincial speech in the Northern and Eastern counties.

173. The function assumed by the glottal plosive in German is replaced in English by a widely developed system of word-binding, or "liaison"; this means that in the same breath-group a terminal consonant bridges the gap between that consonant and a vowel immediately following it, as in *for ever*, *his own*. There is no break in the breath. This linking has preserved the form *an* for *a* before vowels, as in *another*, and accounts for such a form as *newt* for *eft*, and for *an adder* instead of *a nadder*. The question of word-binding in English is treated in the next chapter.[1]

---

[1] Dr Perrett calls my attention to a striking example of linking in an Old High German poem: "In the O.H.G. *Ludwigslied* we find *wolar abur* with the r-link as hiatus-filler between vowels of like quality". It is necessary to point out, however, that the poem is written in the Rhenish-Franconian dialect.

XI

WORD-BINDING AND GLIDES

174. Within a breath-group, consonant-sounds, as we have just pointed out, are carried on into the vowel-sounds following them. But when two vowel-sounds come together in a breath-group, a glide is inserted. This glide is a very faint j sound after a front vowel or ɔɪ, a very weak w after a back vowel containing u in any form, as aʊ and oᵘ. Examples: *he answered* (hiʲɑːnsɜˑd), *the enemy* (ðiʲɛnəmì), *lay out* (leʲaʊt), *Iona* (aɪʲoᵘnɜ), *enjoying*; *who are you* (huʷɑːju), *however, no end* (noʷɛnd), *to answer* (tuʷɑːnsɜ).[1] Written *r* reasserts itself in word-binding; cf. *bear* (bɛɜ) with *bearable* (bɛərəbl). After ɔː from written *aw*, and ɑː from *a*, illiterate speakers often insert r by analogy with ɔː from *or* and ɑː from *ar*, as in *I sawr 'im, papar an' mamma*. The case of ər from written *a* has already been dealt with in § 128.

175. Welshmen generally make these glides too distinct, and a binding consonant too forcible. They therefore make little

[1] These glides must not be made distinct, even in emphatic speech. In a gramophone record spoken by Professor Daniel Jones, of all people, there is a striking instance of this. In an anecdote of a man who was ill and had to take a very black-looking medicine, his servant one day gave him some ink instead of his medicine. When he saw what he had done he exclaimed, "I beg your pardon, sir, but I have given you ink instead of your medicine". This comes out distinctly in the record as "I have given you wink...". Apart from the exaggeration of the glide, this is good proof that the glide is here a definite feature of St. E. in such a position. Many foreign speakers who have no such word-linking in their own tongue, have the greatest difficulty in inserting it where it is customary in Southern E., and the consequent break in the continuity of the breath, even though unaccompanied by a glottal plosive, sounds foreign to an English ear. In the example just given, it should be impossible to hear where *you* ends and *ink* begins, though at the first blush it may sound like rank heresy to postulate this.

or no difference between *this ink* and *this sink*. A Welsh clergy-
man has been heard to read the tenth commandment: "Thou
shalt not covet thy neighbour's wife, nor his sox, nor his sass,
nor anything that is siss".

176. Owing to the agency of word-binding, words are normally run together to such an extent that several of them in
one sentence may sound like a single word. Thus, in "I don't
know who put the idea into his head", there are four sound-
groups; anyone who was unacquainted with English, but who
could transcribe phonetically, might write it down in this way:
aɪˈdoᵘntno huːputðiaɪ diᴣɪntuɪz hɛˑd. Phonetically viewed, the
spoken language really consists of a series of breath-groups, not
of a number of isolated words. Many foreigners have difficulty
in realizing this.

177. Now what shall we say to the old pedagogic formula,
"Don't run your words together; pronounce each word distinctly!"? If we were to follow this injunction we should give
each word its pronunciation as an isolated unit, we should omit
a number of essential glides, we should substitute full vowel-
sounds for weak or obscured ones, and do other things calculated
to produce an unnatural or pedantic effect. Unless we run our
words together we shall deprive the stressed vowels of their
prominence in breath-groups, and give unstressed vowels an
importance that may obscure or ruin the sense.

178. The dictionary pronunciation of many common words
(see §§ 145 *seq.*) is the emphatic form of these words, which is
rare in connected speech. A dictionary may tell you that the
definite article is pronounced ðiː, whereas its normal form is ði
before a vowel, and ðə before a consonant, as in *the old* (ði oᵘld)
and *the young* (ðə jʌŋ). *Have* (hæˑv) may become həv, əv or v in
connected speech, the form hæˑv only occurring when the word

is stressed. *To* is generally tə before a consonant, tu before a vowel: *there's nothing to be said, nothing to add*. The foreign student is often prone to give a word its spelling pronunciation, his visual memory being so much keener than his auditive one. Thus, when a Frenchman hears the words *he had lost it* pronounced hiˑd lɔˑstɪt, and fails to grasp the meaning, you have only to show him the written words and he at once understands, to the joyful accompaniment of, "Ah, je comprends: iː ad lost iˑt". This tendency—to give each word equal value—produces a staccato effect on an English ear, however well the phones may be articulated. Until this defect is remedied, the English thus pronounced will always sound incorrect. One of the greatest difficulties that foreigners have in speaking English or reading it aloud, is to invest the more important words in a breath-group with individuality without isolating them. The important words must not be made emphatic, or given too prominent a place in the sentence, and the unimportant ones should be treated as proclitic or enclitic, i.e. attached so closely to a following word or a preceding word as to have no separate accent.

XII

ASSIMILATION

179. Assimilation, which means the influence or effect of one sound upon a neighbouring one, plays a great part in the sound-groups of all languages. The commonest instances of assimilation in English can be heard in the plurals of substantives and the 3rd person singular of the present tense in verbs, where a voiced sound is followed by a voiced consonant, a voiceless one by a voiceless. Examples: *bid, bids* (bɪd, bɪdz),

cut, cuts (kʌt, kʌts), *rob, robs* (rɒb, rɒbz), *drop, drops* (drɒp, drɒps), *stay, stays* (steⁱ, steⁱz), *state, states* (steⁱt, steⁱts), *stare, stares* (stɛɜ, stɛɜˑz).

180. In some adverbs assimilation has never taken place, as in *once, twice, else, hence, whence,* from Old English *ānes, twiges, elles, hennes, whennes;* also in *since.* In the verbal forms *felt, learnt, burnt, meant, dreamt* and *dealt,* note the actual development of a voiceless consonant at the end, on the analogy of such pairs as *build built, send sent, gird girt,* in which the *t* of the past tense represents an older ending *-te* from *-de.* In *used to* (juˑst tʊ), meaning "made a practice of", the st has developed from zd by assimilation with the t of the *to* that always follows it in this sense.

181. Some cases of assimilation have already been touched on in §§ 112 and 113. A few more may be mentioned in this place.

A very common cause of assimilation is exemplified in such a word as *horseshoe.* The tongue assumes the position for the ʃ in *shoe* too quickly, so that the s in *horse* becomes ʃ, and ʃʃ results.

182. In many other compounds stressed on the first element, assimilation has resulted in changing the spoken forms of words: in *newspaper* zp has become sp, in *raspberry* spb has become sb and then zb, in *gooseberry* sb has become zb, in *cupboard* the pb has become b, and in *handkerchief* ndk has developed through nk to ŋk. In *issue* all three forms ɪsjù, ɪʃjù and ɪʃù exist in current speech.

183. The important development of ʧ from older tj, and of ʃ from older sj, as in *nature* (neⁱʧɛ), *nation* (neⁱʃn), date back to the beginning of the seventeenth century. In unaffected speech there is a tendency to turn every tj into ʧ, and every dj into ʤ,

especially before u or ʊ, as in *I'll meet you, would you mind*...;
but the plosive tʃ for tj is avoided by careful speakers, who
employ an intermediate form, which is practically tç, i.e.
assimilation takes place, and the result is such a pronunciation
as aɪl miˑtçù. A similar compromise is heard in the *tj* of Swedish
tjäna (cf. § 112).

184. A good example of assimilation is heard in the pronunciation of the word *eighth*, where the t of the eⁱtθ, owing to
the predental fricative that follows it, becomes predental instead of postdental (cf. §§ 21 and 131). All the more remarkable
is the persistence of dθ in the words *width* and *breadth*, where the
assimilative attraction has failed to force its way into careful
speech; possibly the spelling has played its part here in pre-
serving the dθ, or else the words merely exemplify the extra-
ordinary conservatism of English consonant-sounds. The student
of languages need only call to mind the present English pronunciation of *faith*, which has preserved a consonant-sound[1]
that was sounded in Old French about a thousand years ago.

185. Before the velar plosives k and g, n is frequently dis-
placed by ŋ in a stressed syllable, as in *conquer, conger*, but when
the stressed syllable follows the n it is best to avoid assimilation,
as in *enquire* (ɪnˈkwaɪə rather than ɪŋˈkwaɪə). Even in the
stressed syllable assimilation is not consistently carried out:
by some speakers *income* is pronounced ɪnkəm, by others ɪŋkəm.

186. In rapid colloquial speech, innumerable cases of assimilation can be heard, but foreign speakers should be chary of
imitating them. Many of these cases, however, belong rather
to the domain of elision and simplification, and are discussed in
the chapter that follows.

[1] Though it has become unvoiced in English. (Note communicated by
Professor Jespersen.)

In dialect speech the nasalizing of a vowel under the influence of a nasal consonant is also a form of assimilation, the vowel most easily affected being apparently aɪ, as in *night time*. The worst offenders in this respect are cockneys and Birmingham people (cf. § 90, note 2). In American speech, nasalizing is common, and when very strong it is an unpleasant feature of American E. But most Americans are quite unconscious of the fact that they nasalize at all.

XIII

ELISION AND SIMPLIFICATION

187. In colloquial speech the simplification of difficult groups of consonants is carried very far, as in the rapid pronunciation of *bread and butter* (brɛd n bʌtə), *cup and saucer* (kʌp m sɔˑsə), *cold-blooded* (koᵘlblʌdɪd), *grandfather* (grænfɑːðə), while clipped forms of words are frequent, as in præps for *perhaps* (pəhæps). But in many words this simplification has been extended to careful speech as well, as in *castle* (kɑːsl), *apostle* (əpɒsl), *soften* (sɔˑfn), *Wednesday* (wɛnzdɪ), *handsome* (hænsəm), *towards* (tɔːdz), *Marylebone* (mærɪbən) beside the fuller mærɪlɪboᵘn, *Marjoribanks* (mɑːʃbæŋks) and a considerable number of other names. In the category of surnames and place-names, the foreigner must always be prepared to meet with surprises, as when he discovers that *Beauchamp* is biːtʃəm; *Cockburn*, koᵘbən; *Colquhoun*, kəhuːn; *Raleigh*, rɔːlɪ; *Legh*, liː; *Bohun*, buːn; *Bideford*, bɪdɪfəd; *Malpas*, maupəs; *Menai*, mɛnɪ; *Mousehole*, mauzl; *Ludgvan*, lʌdʒn; *Gloucester*, glɒstə; *Leicester*, lɛstə; *Worcester*, wustə; *Isleworth*, aɪzlwɜˑθ; *Islington*, ɪzlɪŋtən; *Flitwick*, flɪtɪk; *Dulwich*, dʌlɪdʒ; *Loughborough*, lʌfbərə; and *Slough*, slau : to take

a score of them at random. In several family-names, more than one pronunciation exists; *Pepys* of Diary fame is generally called pi·ps, but others with the same name call themselves pɛps or pɛpɪs; *Cassilis* is usually kæslz, but the Leicestershire "Cassilises" pronounce their name as it is spelt.

188. For some words in which simplification of awkward groups of consonants has been adopted in St. E., as in *chestnut* (ʧɛsnʌt), some dictionaries persist in retaining older pronunciations, justified by dialect or colonial speech, but no longer used in St. E. It must always be remembered, however, that if dictionaries gave the pronunciation of words as they are sounded in St. E., they would reproduce the speech of a mere fraction of the English-speaking world: the hundred million inhabitants of U.S.A., for instance, would find that it differed in at least 30 per cent. of the words from the forms they employ. This is why transcribed pronunciations are generally given in such a Broad form that they are capable of more than one interpretation; even purely pronouncing dictionaries give less exact transcriptions than is desirable.

With regard to the simplification of difficult consonant-groups, and the forms of words as they appear in colloquial English, the student should therefore make a point of studying good phonetic texts of recent date. Most of these texts record the natural pronunciation of words as read or spoken by educated speakers. Rapid conversation tolerates so much elision and simplification that transcriptions of it would confuse rather than benefit the foreign student.

189. Even among careful speakers, diversity may be heard in the pronunciation of some consonant-groups, noticeably in ʧ and ʤ when they stand finally after n, as in *punch, inch, singe, sponge*; in these words nʧ and nʤ now sound old-fashioned, the

present forms being generally ɪnʃ, etc. But the plosives ʧ and ʤ generally persist after n when a syllable follows; streˈnʒ beside streˈnʤ is unobjectionable, but streˈnʒɛ for *stranger* is not the St. E. form. For *revenge* we may bracket rɪˈvɛnʒ and rɪˈvɛnʤ, but only allow the form vɛnʤəns for *vengeance*. Some speakers change ʧ and ʤ to ʃ and ʒ after l, and say fɪlʃ for *filch* (fɪlʧ) and bʌlʒ for bʌlʤ (*bulge*), but this is not to be recommended.

190. Some consonant-groups persist where we might expect simplification, as in the combination ndð in *and the...*, though in quick speech the d is generally dropped. Note also the retention by some of the t before θ in *sixth* (sɪkstθ), *sixthly* (sɪkstθlɪ), despite the difficult consonant-groups that present themselves.

191. Many foreign speakers omit the g after ŋ in *England*,[1] *finger*, *language*, which are ɪŋglənd, fɪŋgɜ, læŋgwɪʤ, but the phonetic transcript soon breaks them of the habit.

XIV

DIFFICULT SOUNDS IN ENGLISH

192. If you ask a foreigner to mention difficult sounds in English, he will very likely mention the *th* sounds. Actually these are easily acquired, once the tongue-position has been grasped. Then ask him if the word *yes* is difficult. He will probably answer "No". There are only three sounds in it, and they are apparently easy to produce. Yet the word is frequently mispronounced by foreign speakers. The Swede can, and often

---

[1] The forms ɛŋglənd and ɛŋglɪʃ recently affected by a few speakers who ought to know better, are intolerable; the historic sound-shift to ɪ in these instances is too well rooted to be ousted by such adventitious substitutes.

does, make three mistakes in saying it: the blade of his tongue
is too high for the j, which becomes ᵈj; the ɛ is too tense and too
long; the s is not hissed enough, and sounds like ᶎ. The first
of these mistakes can often be heard in his pronunciation of the
substantive *use*, which then becomes like *deuce* or even *juice*.
The tongue must have the position it reaches for the main part
of the iː in *three*; so it is in the right position for the j in the
combinations *three young men, three years*.

193. Let us take another example of apparent simplicity,
where there are underlying difficulties. From the transcribed
forms of *this* and *these* (ðɪs and ðiːz), and the principles de-
ducible from them, we can state: the vowel in *this* is short and
lax, in *these* it is long and tense; the end consonant in *this* is
both voiceless and long, whereas in *these* it is voiced half-way
through, and shortened. Not quite so simple as the uninitiated
might imagine! And the consequence is that such a pair is
almost invariably mispronounced by foreigners. In the pair
that, those the more radical change of vowel-sound helps to
obscure the fault or faults that may be made in articulating the
words.

194. Apparent difficulties may, however, be phonetic difficulties as well. Difficult consonant-groups occur frequently in
English, especially when hissing and lisping sounds come together. Thus, we have awkward groups of consonants that are
hard to articulate clearly in *what's that* (wɒts ðæt), *clothes*
(kloᵘðz), *the sixth sense* (ðə sɪkstθ sɛns)—with more troublesome
consonant-sounds than even Russian can boast of—*the Smiths
themselves* (ðə smɪθs ðəmsɛlvz), "*Breathes there the man with soul
so dead*" (briːðz ðɛðə), *he stocks shot-silk socks with spots, I'm sure
she sells sea-shore shells*.

195. Trouble can sometimes be caused through the letters of

the alphabet having different values in different languages. The German *w* has the value of **v**, which helps to encourage a confusion between **v** and **w** in a German's pronunciation of English. This was once a characteristic of cockney speech, as readers of *Pickwick* can see; thus, *winegar* for *vinegar*, *weal* for *veal*; but this ceased to be a cockney fault *c.* 1850.

196. With the **v** sound, speakers with a variety that differs from the English **v** in mode of production must be careful to master the new sound. Whereas English **v** is produced by a loose lower lip in contact with the upper teeth, the Dutch often use a bi-labial consonant, symbol ʋ,[1] the lips being just in contact and drawn back; the effect resembles English **w** rather than **v**. The Norwegian sound that is produced with a stiff lower lip is quite un-English.

197. English **w** is produced with lips rounded about as much as for sounding the vowel uː. In imitating the English consonant, foreign speakers often substitute the vowel u for initial **w**. The French even write it as a vowel: *ouest, Cornouailles*. This is not, of course, identical with the true **w** sound. To articulate the latter, put the lips in position for uː, then draw them back energetically, using voice; but voicing must not begin before the lips are being drawn back, or a vowel will result.

198. Many foreigners find difficulty in sounding a **g** before the n of a following syllable, and owing to assimilation of these sounds in their own language, make ŋn of the combination, as in *Agnes, signal, cognate*. An infinitesimal pause after the **g** helps to correct this; thus, mæg-ˈnɪfɪsn̩t, sɪg-n̩l̩.

199. The absence of the tonic accent in French makes a Germanic tongue difficult for French speakers to master. How

---

[1] Professor Daniel Jones informs me that β is now substituted for ʋ when referring to this sound.

a Frenchman's pronunciation can be misinterpreted in consequence of faulty stressing is well illustrated by the story of the Frenchman who had given the waiter an order for *potatoes*, and was served with *buttered toast*. Until he has mastered the hammer-beat of the English tonic accent, a Frenchman will fail to pronounce English correctly. Moreover, he must get into the way of partially unvoicing final voiced consonants, which he usually voices throughout; otherwise he will make the plosive element of his b, d, ʤ, g a faint murmur, and in consequence make the word *lad* sound much like *ladder*. Italians and Japanese are prone to support all final consonants, and even a consonant-sound at the end of a syllable that is not followed by a vowel in the same breath-group.

200. The doubled consonant-sounds, so innumerable in Italian, as in *bello*, *anello*, *troppo*, *freddo*, are very rare in English; a doubled consonant can be heard in *unknown*, or in *wholly* as opposed to *holy*; usually when a doubled letter is written it is pronounced as a single sound, though sometimes lengthened, as in *illegal*.

201. Of consonant-sounds, apart from those already dealt with, which diverge markedly from the normal English sound, I may mention the ʃ used by many Swedes. This differs from the English ʃ in that the blade of the tongue, which is chiefly instrumental in forming the sound, is retracted and the sound becomes a palatal instead of a postdental fricative. The passage for the sound is consequently made much more open than the one requisite for articulating St. E. ʃ, and the sound itself becomes less distinct. The difference between the two might be illustrated by comparing the noise emitted by the piston of a locomotive with that of its funnel. Swedes who normally use such an ʃ sound, generally employ a supradental ṣ for written

rs (see § 126), and this makes quite a good substitute for the English ʃ.

202. Some speakers of St. E. produce ʃ with the tip instead of the blade of the tongue, the tip being curled slightly upwards. Others, again, who use the blade for its production, lower the tip of the tongue towards, or even to touch, the lower teeth. These differences seem to make no appreciable difference in the quality of the sound produced.

The English tongue-position may also be varied slightly according to the vowel that follows ʃ, so that the ʃ is more advanced for a front than for a back vowel. But there always remains distinct friction between tongue and gums, and against the front teeth.

203. The quality of ʃ may, however, be slightly affected by the extent to which the lips are protruded and rounded. The typical St. E. ʃ is produced with very little protrusion or rounding compared with the normal French and German ʃ sounds. But here, too, the vowel following may influence the shape of the lips in English, so that before a rounded vowel there may be some rounding in anticipation of the sound to come, whereas before an unrounded vowel there may appear to be no rounding whatever; but there is always some tensing of the lips.

Should a very forward ʃ be used before a back vowel, a glide tends to insert itself between these two sounds. The tense ʃ of Dutchmen and Danes induces a glide in this case, and hence they so often say ʃjɔːt instead of ʃɔːt for *short*, and tʃjuːz for tʃuːz (*choose*).

204. Those Swedes who use supradental t, d, s, l and n may be reminded that these sounds recall the corresponding consonants in English, all five being postdental sounds in Standard speech.

XV

DIALECT FORMS

205. The foreign student with some phonetic training can pass on from the study of St. E. to a systematic study of a dialect; this will help to train the ear still more sharply in differentiating between closely related sounds. For Northern E. generally the best introduction is Richard Lloyd's *Northern English: Phonetics, Grammar, Texts*.

206. Some of the common varieties of spoken English can be gathered from the transcription of an everyday word in its different forms. If we take the plural of *flower*, we have flaʊ3z in St. E., flaũ3z in American E., flæʊ3z in refined cockney, flæːz or flaːz in broad cockney, fluːrz in the Glasgow dialect, vlaʊ3z in Devonian, etc. To indicate some of the other dialectal divergences from Standard speech we may require other modifiers or new symbols. Thus, for the ɑː in *father* cockney speech has a lowered ɑː, symbol Aː. This Aː is sometimes accompanied by lip-rounding, and then hardly differs from ɔː. Aː for ɑː is common in unrefined speech on the west coast of Sweden around Gothenburg, where *dag* "day" may be heard pronounced with a vowel-sound that is almost as low as the ɒ in English *dog*.

207. We may occasionally find it necessary to record lowered or raised varieties of sounds. The lowered 3ː, symbol 3ᵥː, is common in the cockney pronunciation of *bird*, *hurt*, etc. The raised variety of 3ː, symbol 3ᴗː, is the "minced" form used by some speakers, especially by ladies, as in *pearl*, with spreading of the lips, hence pᵌᶜᴗːl.

208. Another device, which is of practical use in transcribing new sounds, is to place a small letter after a symbol to show

that the sound approximates to the one represented by the smaller letter. Thus, in Swedish an ʃ is often heard which approximates to ç, as in the word *maskin* (maʃᶜiːn). If this sound were used for the ʃ in the English word *machine*, it would give the effect of faulty articulation due to a physical cause.

209. Other devices may be employed as occasion requires. Whispered sounds can be indicated by placing a comma below the whispered sound, as in the normal pronunciation of *band* (bænːd̦). The transcription pu̦t for *put* would indicate that the whole word is whispered. The necessity for this seldom arises in transcribing normal English speech.

210. Advanced, retracted, raised and lowered varieties of sounds are marked by using the modifiers ˖, ˗, ˔, ˕, respectively, after the sound.

English t and d, as we have pointed out, are normally t˗ and d˗, or postdental; but before θ or ð they become predental, as in *eighth* (eⁱtθ), *and then* (ænd ðɛn). The Devonian form of *poodle* may be transcribed pu˖ːdl, to distinguish it from the St. E. form.

211. Other modifiers have already been introduced in previous sections. Generally speaking, modifiers should be used sparingly, as they tend to disfigure the phonetic transcription. On the other hand, a judicious use of them often enables one to avoid employing symbols that are not easily written, such as inverted a.

XVI

INTONATION

212. A problem that has troubled phoneticians very considerably is how to devise a practical system of marking intonation, i.e. the modulation of the voice in speaking. Intonation curves are expensive to print, and musical notes have proved unsatisfactory. One of the best methods of marking both stress and intonation has been devised by Klinghardt in his *Übungen im englischen Tonfall*, to which students may be referred for a full treatment of the intonation of St. E. Even Klinghardt's system of marking intonation occupies a good deal of space. Most transcriptions omit intonation-marks altogether, or content themselves with giving occasional intonation-marks in the text, so as to show, for instance, falling, rising, or falling-rising intonation. But such a simple plan can only give very vague information. We can say the word *yes* starting from a medium and falling to a low pitch when we wish to make a conclusive affirmation; *yes* going from high to low pitch is emphatically conclusive; rising from low to medium it is encouraging; from low to high it indicates a dubious attitude on the part of the speaker; while *yes* with medium-low-medium intonation indicates qualified assent.

213. Generally speaking, the falling tone is affirmative or conclusive, the rising tone interrogative or expectant. But complete questions containing a specific interrogative word are treated as statements, e.g. *Where are you* \?, *What's the matter* \?, *When did he come* \ ? Rhetorical questions are put with falling intonation: *It's a fine day, isn't it* \? Compare with these the rising tone in *What's that* / ?, *Are you coming* / ?, *Is that the only*

one / ? A rising tone often shows that a statement or command will be followed by an additional statement: *Don't speak to him now* / , *he's busy*. A falling tone is used for the last of two or more alternative questions: *Will you take milk* / , *or lemonade* / , *or coffee* \ ?, *Was it John* / , *or Henry* \ ? To put rising tone on *Henry* would suggest that another alternative is suggested, though not expressed. Statements or commands uttered with rising tone soften them down, make them less emphatic, or throw some doubt into them: *He promised to come, didn't he?*, *Well, he promised* / . . . . A falling tone may indicate impatience, sarcasm, or the like: *Are you ready* \ ? Unusually high pitch often marks surprise: *Five hundred pounds*, with high pitch on *Five*. Unusually low pitch may mark contempt, or a similar emotion: *He offered him a penny!*, *He thinks he's ill!* with low tone on *penny* and *ill*.

214. The unexpected tone, which may be infinitely varied, betrays some emotional feeling on the part of the speaker. The pitch, indeed, varies according to the intensity of feeling behind the words. But extreme variations in the pitch of the voice are unusual in English, save in dramatic or oratorical declamation.

Where a comma is used in an English text, the most common tone on the word that precedes it is a rising one, especially if the comma merely separates a dependent clause from its principal one, or separates adjectives qualifying the same noun: *Whether he returned or not* / , *I never heard. An odious* / , *stingy* / , *hard* / , *unfeeling man*.

215. It must always be remembered that the human voice does not jump from one note to another, but runs up or down the scale; hence musical notes are unsatisfactory for showing intonation: the notes only mark stages in the musical intonation.

Intonation curves printed on a musical stave[1] are the most perfect method of reproducing the intonation of the voice in speaking, but it is such complicated printing that simpler methods must be adopted. Klinghardt's dotted lines, with larger dots to mark the stresses, are sufficiently accurate, and are easily interpreted.

216. It is only recently that serious attention has been given to intonation, and much still remains to be done, especially in the study of dialect intonation. When English intonation is spoken of in books, the intonation referred to is usually that of speakers of St. E. Such an intonation can, of course, be compared with a typical French or German intonation. From such a point of view general tendencies can easily be observed, and are fairly well known.

217. Thus, the upward inflection or glide in the tone when a word is followed by a slight pause, and the downward inflection to mark the close of a sentence, which are so common in English, are practically unknown in French or German. In *that's his son* the down-glide coincides with the end-consonant in *son*; in *he was going out, though it was so late*... the up-glide in the word *out* coincides with the second element of the diphthong aʊ, since it can leave no trace on the final plosive t. In French and German the pitch of the voice would be considerably higher on such a word than in English, but would have no up-glide. In Swedish, before a pause the normal intonation is to run up the scale, so that in such a position the word *skolgosse* would be intoned (. · ˙).

Again, whereas the concluding word in an English statement will begin with an only slightly lower pitch than the preceding

---

[1] But without a clef mark, since it is relative, not absolute pitch that matters.

word, and end on a down-glide, the German word would have a considerably lower pitch to begin with, and sustain it to the end; in French, where the tone would naturally be rising up to the last word, the drop to the pitch of the final syllable would be a whole octave, or even more.

218. Most people, when speaking a foreign language, use much the same intonation as when they are speaking their own. But any foreign intonation that sounds strange to an English ear, however well the words are articulated, seriously detracts from the otherwise good impression such a pronunciation would produce. This is the case with Swedes who have a pronouncedly Swedish intonation; the isolated English words cause them comparatively few difficulties, and yet the sing-song Swedish intonation catches the English ear. It is very exceptionally that their characteristic compound tone, falling-rising, so often heard in dissyllabic and polysyllabic words in Swedish, occurs in English; we may use it for special emphasis occasionally, as in *I couldn't go myself* ∨, *but*..., whereas in Swedish it may affect the meaning of a word: *gripen*, "the grip", has simple tone, but *gripen*, "gripped", has compound tone. In English, intonation does not affect the meaning of a word, though it may modify the sense of an expression: *Good morning!* is spoken with falling intonation on meeting a person, with falling-rising on parting with him; *I beg your pardon*, spoken with rising intonation on *pardon*, means "What did you say?", while with level or falling intonation it means "I'm sorry".

The finer details of intonation can conveniently be studied by means of good gramophone records, with a printed text before the eyes.

219. The upward and downward inflections in tone used in Standard speech are often so slight as to be almost inaudible;

to represent them by a curved line is very misleading, as the foreign student invariably exaggerates these glides when he sees them so represented. If a dot be used to stand for a syllable, and larger dots be used for the stressed syllables, all that is required in many cases is to use a comma in place of a dot for the down-glide, and an inverted comma for the up-glide. This may be exemplified from p. 158 in Klinghardt's book:

A well-known dramatist

was once away in the country

when he unexpectedly received

an anxious letter from his wife.

220. A common fault made by foreigners in speaking English is to raise the pitch of the voice on a strongly stressed sound, often producing on the English ear an effect of surprise or over-emphasis.

221. Foreign speakers with excessive musical deviation from the normal English type, i.e. with foreign modulation, can be corrected with tolerable success by being made to start the reading of each sentence on a somewhat higher pitch than their normal one, and to let the pitch drop very slightly as the sentence proceeds. The whole interval should not exceed an octave. It may sound at first something like a caricature of English intonation, but it will help to break the student of the habit of using his native intonation in reading from an English text.

222. In the speech of a Frenchman the natural tendency is to keep running up the scale; English intonation is inclined to do just the reverse. A page of French intonation therefore resembles a number of waves rising each to its crest, and a page of English intonation represents the waves toppling down again.

223. Although there is considerable truth in the assertion

that an Englishman's natural intonation borders on steady monotony, it must be remembered that much depends on the individual speaker, and that, just as no two individuals pronounce exactly alike, no two individuals have exactly the same intonation. But intonation varies more from county to county than the way in which the phones are articulated, great as these latter differences may be. In a stimulating chapter on "Race and Language",[1] Mr Anthony Collett remarks: "...the traces of the diverse ancient speeches linger in the talk of thousands or even millions of modern English people who have abandoned most of the old dialect words. The way in which the vowels are sounded is more persistent than a vocabulary, and intonation is most ineradicable of all...". "The 'Suffolk whine' is an intonation as marked as the sing-song of the Welsh border, and precisely its opposite, for it droops at the end of a sentence like the wail of a deflated bagpipe. An officer tells how when marching in the Egyptian desert a Norfolk battalion would imitate the Suffolk intonation as the sister unit passed; exile and tedium were lightened for both by the familiar gibe".[2]

224. Foreign students with a sharp sense of hearing often acquire a tolerably good English intonation by merely imitating the teacher; in extremely stubborn cases I have found it a good plan to read to the pupil a passage in his own language, but with an English intonation. His first impulse is to laugh at the teacher, but he often ends in wondering to himself why the teacher does not laugh at him.

[1] Anthony Collett, *The Changing Face of England* (Nisbet: London, 1926), p. 234.
[2] *Ibid.* p. 239.

BIBLIOGRAPHY

STORM, JOHAN, *Englische Philologie* (Reisland: Leipzig, 1892–96). Vol. I mentions or reviews practically everything of importance written about English phonetics up to 1892.

Since 1892 valuable contributions to the phonetics of English have been made by RICHARD LLOYD, HENRY SWEET, OTTO JESPERSEN, WALTER RIPMAN, and DANIEL JONES. The *Pronouncing Dictionary* of the last named should be collated with other works, such as *The Standard Dictionary* (Funk and Wagnalls: New York), J. A. AFZELIUS, *A Concise Pronouncing Dictionary of Modern English* (Norstedt: Stockholm, 1909). *The Concise Dictionary of Current English* and *The Pocket Oxford Dictionary* (Oxford Univ. Press).

Phonetic texts have been written by SWEET, LAURA SOAMES, R. LLOYD, D. JONES, W. RIPMAN, L. E. ARMSTRONG, E. R. EDWARDS, G. E. FUHRKEN, C. M. RICE, G. NOEL-ARMFIELD, and others; but very much still remains to be done in this domain.

For intonation, the student may consult ARMSTRONG-WARD, *Handbook of English Intonation* (Heffer), H. E. PALMER, *English Intonation* (Heffer), or KLINGHARDT und KLEMM, *Übungen im englischen Tonfall* (Schulze: Cöthen); for quantity, E. A. MEYER, *Englische Lautdauer* (Harrasowitz: Leipzig); for dialectal, provincial and local speech, IDA C. WARD, *The Phonetics of English* (Heffer); for American pronunciation, G. P. KRAPP, *The Pronunciation of Standard English in America* (Oxford Univ. Press); for comparative phonetics, PAUL PASSY's tabloid volume, *Petite Phonétique Comparée* (Teubner), and W. VIETOR's *Kleine Phonetik* in the English edition by RIPMAN (Dent); for the practical study of languages, the volume with that title by SWEET (Dent); for sound-changes in English, JESPERSEN, *A Modern English Grammar*, Part I (Winter: Heidelberg), and R. E. ZACHRISSON, *Pronunciation of English Vowels* 1400–1700 (Wettergren and Kerber: Göteborg); for instrumental phonetics, E. W. SCRIPTURE, *Elements of Experimental Phonetics* (New York); for voice production, BERNARD MACDONALD, *English Speech To-day* (Allen and Unwin);

8-2

for simplified spelling, the pamphlets of the two societies, Simplified Spelling Society and Simplified Spelling Board (44, Great Russel Street, London), and R. E. ZACHRISSON's *Anglic* (Anglic Fund: Uppsala); for simplified transcript, WILFRID PERRETT, *Peetickay* (Heffer), and EDGAR JACOT, *La Prononciation anglaise systématisée* (Jacot: Neuchâtel); and for a suggestive essay on local speech, Chapter VIII in ANTHONY COLLETT's *The Changing Face of England* (Nisbet).

INDEX OF SUBJECTS AND PHONETIC TERMS

(The figures refer to the paragraphs)

INDEX OF SOUNDS, SYMBOLS
AND DIACRITIC SIGNS

(The figures refer to the paragraphs)

The following is the alphabetical order of the symbols used in this book:

ɑ A a aɪ aɪɜ aʊ aʊɜ æ b ç d ʤ ð eⁱ ɛ ɛɜ ə ɜ œ f g h i ɪ ɪ̀ ɪɜ j k l m n ŋ oᵘ
ɒ ɔ ɔɪ p r ʀ ʁ s ʃ t ʧ θ u ù ʊ ʊɜ ʌ v w ʍ x z ʒ ʔ.

ˈ before a syllable indicates the chief stress
ˌ before a syllable indicates the secondary stress
˝ over a vowel indicates an obscured vowel-sound
ˋ over a vowel indicates a lowered variety of the sound
ˊ over a vowel indicates a raised variety of the sound
ː after a vowel indicates full length
˙ after a vowel indicates half length
ᵢ under a liquid indicates that it is syllabic
₀ under a consonant indicates that it is unvoiced
ʰ after a consonant indicates the aspiration following it
⊢ after a symbol indicates that the sound is advanced
⊣ after a symbol indicates that the sound is retracted
⊥ after a symbol indicates that the sound is raised
⊤ after a symbol indicates that the sound is lowered
, under a symbol indicates whisper
. under a vowel indicates that it is cacuminal
˜ over a vowel indicates nasalizing
ɔ after a symbol indicates that the sound is rounded
ᶜ after a symbol indicates that the sound is spoken with spread lips
╱ indicates rising intonation
╲ indicates falling intonation
∨ indicates falling-rising intonation
> indicates a clear beginning

For EU product safety concerns, contact us at Calle de José Abascal, 56–1°,
28003 Madrid, Spain or eugpsr@cambridge.org.

www.ingramcontent.com/pod-product-compliance
Ingram Content Group UK Ltd.
Pitfield, Milton Keynes, MK11 3LW, UK
UKHW012333130625
459647UK00009B/255